LIGHT PANZERS

OSPREY
PUBLISHING

LIGHT PA

ANZERS

Thomas Anderson

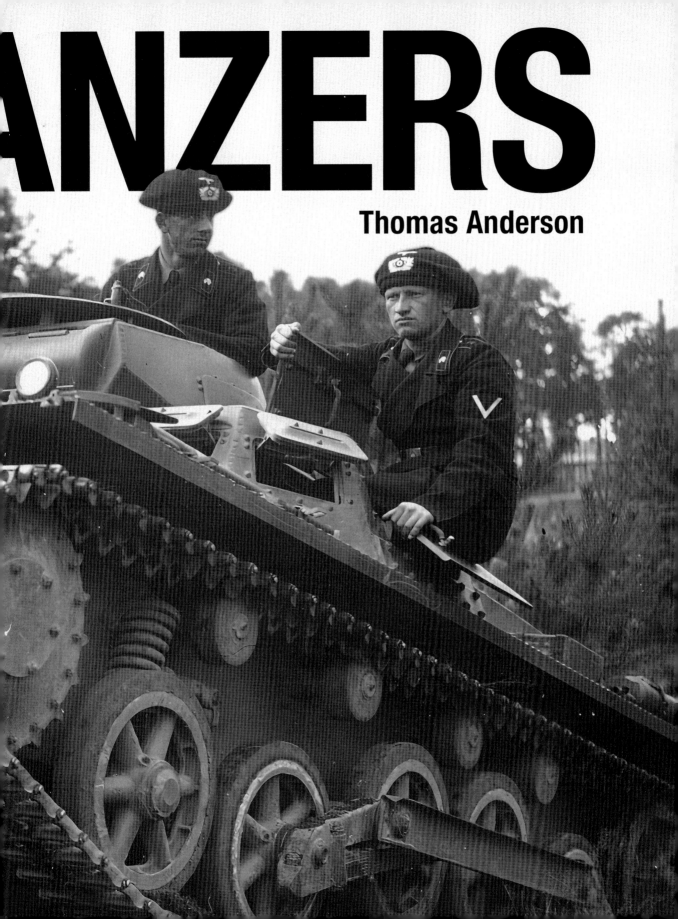

OSPREY PUBLISHING
Bloomsbury Publishing Plc
Kemp House, Chawley Park, Cumnor Hill,
Oxford OX2 9PH, UK
29 Earlsfort Terrace, Dublin 2, Ireland
1385 Broadway, 5th Floor, New York, NY 10018, USA
E-mail: info@ospreypublishing.com
www.ospreypublishing.com

OSPREY is a trademark of Osprey Publishing Ltd

First published in Great Britain in 2025

ISBN: HB 9781472861771
eBook 9781472861764
ePDF 9781472861795
XML 9781472861788

25 26 27 28 29 10 9 8 7 6 5 4 3 2 1

Conceived and edited by Jasper Spencer-Smith
Page Layout: Justin Smith
Jacket design: Stewart Larking
Index: Michael Napier
Produced for Bloomsbury Publishing Plc
by Editworks Limited

MIX
Paper
FSC   FSC® C047271

Unless otherwise stated, all images are from the author's
collection.
Printed and bound in India by Repro India Ltd.
Osprey Publishing supports the Woodland Trust, the UK's
leading woodland conservation charity.

To find out more about our authors and books visit
www.ospreypublishing.com. Here you will find extracts,
author interviews, details of forthcoming events and the
option to sign up for our newsletter.

CONTENTS

Introduction

Throughout history, military commanders have sought ways to protect their troops from enemy defensive fire. Roman infantry formations carried their shields overhead as protection against arrows, spears and thrown objects. In the medieval period, siege engines carrying a battering ram became roofed to protect those inside.

In the 15th century, Jan Žižka, a Czechoslovak general, deployed a number of horse-drawn war wagons, fitted with firing ports on each side, to achieve success in many battles.

Even the great inventor Leonardo da Vinci (1452–1519) sketched his vision for a multi-gunned armoured fighting vehicle.

Gottfried Wilhelm Leibnitz an inventor in 17th-century Austria, issued his proposal for a 'fire cart', an armoured vehicle powered by what he called a 'gun powder engine' – possibly the forerunner of the internal combustion engine.

In 1903, Leon Lévavasseur, a French artillery officer, issued his proposal for a fully tracked *Canon Autopropulseur* (self-propelled gun) fitted with an armoured superstructure.

The author H. G. Wells wrote an article, 'The Land Ironclads', published in the December 1903 issue of *The Strand* magazine, in which he detailed his ideas, including diagrammatic drawings and sketches, for an armoured fighting vehicle.

In 1911, an officer in the Austrian Army, Günther Berstyn, revealed his design, complete with drawings, for an armoured fighting vehicle that featured a cannon mounted in a rotatable turret. A year later, an Australian civil engineer named Lancelot de Mole prepared his design, supported by a scale model, for a tracked armoured vehicle.

Opposite: A Holt Caterpillar 55hp tractor, with extra-long tracks, being driven up a 10ft bank on the company's testing grounds near the factory in Peoria, Illinois. (NARA)

Nothing came of these projects, possibly due to high-ranking officers' reticence to adopt mechanized support for their infantry and a continuing reliance on horse-mounted cavalry.

At the start of 1914, no military power had large motorized formations and armoured vehicles were almost non-existent. Only France and Russia had wheeled types, which utilized a passenger car or truck chassis fitted with rudimentary armoured bodywork.

Benjamin Holt and Col Ernest Dunlop Swinton, a tracked vehicle specialist from the British Army, outside the premises of the Holt Manufacturing Company in Stockton, California. The one-man Holt Machine Gun Tank was completed too late to be deployed in France. (NARA)

These vehicles were to prove effective, to a certain extent, for suppressing local or national uprisings or cross-border skirmishing with an antagonistic nation. But as far as the battlefield was concerned, both types lacked the necessary cross-country performance.

In order to break the stalemate of almost static trench warfare, a combination of armoured protection, mobility and firepower was indispensable to support an infantry advance.

Tracks, Not Wheels

In the years prior to World War I, two agricultural machinery manufacturers – Holt Manufacturing Company in the US and British company Richard Hornsby & Sons – were developing tracked vehicles. Holt had produced a continuous track tractor and Hornsby had patented their chain track in 1904. In 1910, Holt purchased the Hornsby patent and registered the name Caterpillar as a trademark. In 1925, the company merged with C. L. Best Gas Traction Company to form the Caterpillar Tractor Company.

Both Great Britain and France each had a number of Holt Caterpillar heavy tractors in service by 1914 and most were used for towing heavy artillery pieces. These vehicles would have been readily available for engineers and designers to inspect and evaluate in detail.

Now that they had an effective drive system, work could commence on producing an all-terrain armoured fighting vehicle.

The 1907 Hornsby Chain-Tractor was demonstrated to the British Army as a potential prime mover for heavy artillery. But in 1910, Hornsby sold their patent to Holt, who continued development. (NARA)

Above: Peoria, Illinois: A Holt Caterpillar tractor undergoing trials overseen by representatives of the US Army. (NARA)

Left: A 1917 Holt Caterpillar 5-ton atillery tractor awaiting delivery to the US Army. (NARA)

Light Tank – Origins 1

The company selected to develop and produce the first British tank was William Foster & Company, a Lincoln-based manufacturer of agricultural machinery. Their designers chose to create a rhomboid-shaped tank on which the track followed the outline of the superstructure, but a lack of experience caused them to concentrate more on the positioning of the engine and weaponry than fighting efficiency and crew environment.

The vehicle was built in three versions. A 'Male' type was armed with two Hotchkiss 6-Pounder Quick Firing (QF) guns, both mounted in a sponson attached to either side of the superstructure, and three 0.303in Lewis machine guns. The 'Female' type was designed as a support vehicle and was armed with five 0.303in Lewis machine guns. The third type, the Tank Tender, was produced as an unarmed supplies carrier.

France built two different tank types that utilized a simply modified chassis from a Holt Caterpillar heavy artillery tractor to carry an armoured casemate-type superstructure.

The Schneider *Char* (tank) CA-1 mounted a 75mm Blockhaus Schneider main gun and a ball-mounted 8mm Hotchkiss M1914 machine gun fitted in each side of the body. The much larger St Chamond, meanwhile, was armed with the very effective *Canon de 75mm modèle* 1897 and two 8mm Hotchkiss machine guns. In service, both were designated *Tracteur Blindé de Armé* (armoured weapon armed tractor).

Compared with the British tanks, the French types were nowhere near as sophisticated and had poor cross-country performance, particularly when crossing enemy trenches. Both the Schneider CA-1 and St Chamond failed as combat vehicles.

The mass deployment of British- and French-built tanks on the World War I battlefront had not only a physical, but also a psychological, effect on

Opposite: A7V No.506 *Mephisto* was found abandoned and disabled by troops of the 26th Australian Battalion, Australian Imperial Forces (AIF), when they routed German forces occupying Monument Wood during the Second Battle of Villers-Bretonneux (April 1918). (NARA)

A British Mark (Mk) I being moved forward as troops prepare for an attack on entrenched German forces. The frame-work structure on top of the tank was positioned to prevent hand grenades thrown by German infantry from damaging the thin roof plates.
(NARA)

battle-weary German troops that began to be known to those on the front line as *Panzerschreck* (tank fright).

But as the war continued, these troops noted that the tanks had many mechanical and mobility shortcomings and quickly learned how to deal with the danger. Nevertheless, the deployment of these new fighting machines had to be considered a success: the tank had arrived on the battlefield and did what it was designed to do – break through enemy barbed wire defences and destroy infantry positioned in the myriad deep trenches.

Initially, military planners in the *Deutsche Reich* (German Empire) had an almost pathological aversion to modern technology. However, the reality of the battlefield quickly made it clear that they would have to overcome this and catch up – a seemingly impossible task.

The *Deutsche Reich* was taken by surprise by British and French developments and was late to begin construction of a tracked armoured vehicle. The *Allgemeines-Kriegsdepartement-Abteilung* (A – general war department-section) 7, *Verkehrswesen* (V – transportation), used a tracked chassis taken from a Holt heavy tractor that was on loan from the Austro-Hungarian army.

It was fitted with an armoured casemate-type superstructure, mounted 5.7cm Maxim-Nordenfelt cannon and six 7.92mm *Maschinengewehr* (MG – machine gun) 08. However, as with the French types, the combination of an oversized body mounted on a short and narrow chassis seriously affected cross-country performance.

The first German attempt to build a tank resulted in the A7V *Sturmpanzerwagen* (assault tank). The vehicle, assembled by Daimler-Motoren-Gesellschaft, had a huge casemate-type superstructure and was manned by a commander, a driver, a mechanic, a mechanic/signaller, six MG gunners and six MG loaders, as well as a main gunner and a loader. The driver and commander were seated above the two centrally mounted 101hp Daimler four-cylinder water-cooled engines linked to the transmission on the chassis of a Holt Caterpillar heavy tractor. German engineers had improved the suspension (and fitted protection from shell fire) by using better springing, making the A7V highly mobile on hard-surfaced roads but a complete failure when traversing a heavily cratered battlefield.

The 'Male' version of the Mk I was armed with two Hotchkiss 6-Pounder QF guns mounted in a sponson on each side of the superstructure. Note the extensions fitted to the tracks to improve cross-country mobility. (NARA)

The 'Female' version of the Mk I was armed with machine guns. Here, a later Mk IV is parked in what remains of a French village, as a casualty is loaded into a waiting field ambulance. (NARA)

The A7V was doomed from the beginning. Since no realistic specifications were discussed or issued, the manufacturer had to independently make crucial decisions despite lacking the required technical knowledge. Furthermore, the problem was exacerbated by the British naval blockade, which had severely restricted the supply of essential raw materials to German industry.

On 31 May 1918, a new type of tank entered the World War I battlefield when the French army deployed 30 Renault FT to the Battle of the Aisne. The action was a success despite a lack of heavy tank support.

This new type differed drastically from any previous armoured fighting vehicle: it was relatively small and light and its simple design made it straightforward to assemble, which meant that it was quick and economical to manufacture in large numbers. The vehicle had many features more akin to those of a modern tank: for example, the engine and transmission were fitted in an enclosed compartment in the rear of the hull. This was not only to save space, but also to reduce the impact of engine noise and fumes upon the two-man crew. The type carried either a 37mm Puteaux SA 1918 gun or an

The British military continue develop the Mk I design as the war progressed. The Mk IX was designed as a troop carrier or infantry supply vehicle, but arrived too late to be used on the battlefront.

8mm Hotchkiss machine gun, both operated by the commander and mounted in a turret that could be rotated manually through 360 degrees.

When compared with the types built up until 1918, the Renault FT represented a new class – the light tank – that was fabricated from armour plates impervious to armour-piercing infantry ammunition and which mounted armament that, although light, was feared by trench-bound enemy troops.

The design, mechanical layout and rotatable turret on the FT was to prove groundbreaking and many nations went on to adopt this layout for their tank designs.

Heavier types, such as the British-built Mk I–Mk V tanks, were to be designated medium tanks, while design and development work progressed on even larger, and better armed and armoured, vehicles that would eventually be classified as 'heavy' tanks.

In World War II, although the medium tank became the most important armoured vehicle on the battlefront, the light tank played a vital role in reconnaissance units and for infantry support.

The French-built Schneider CA1 suffered from many design shortcomings. Most importantly, the main armament, a 75mm short-barrelled gun, was mounted on the right-hand side of the casemate-type superstructure. (NARA)

Despite being armed with a powerful 75mm *Canon de modèle* 1897, the St Chamond has to be considered as another failure. The long overhang at the front of the superstructure badly affected cross-country mobility, particularly over heavily cratered terrain. Also, as with the CA 1, the main gun had a very limited traverse. (NARA)

One of the A7V captured after the Battle of Villers-Bretonneux. The German tank, unlike British types, had a sprung running gear that allowed high speeds to be achieved on firm surfaces, but cross-country performance was very poor.
(NARA)

Due to a lack of documents from World War I, it is only possible to speculate as to how German military planners assessed the performance of the A7V after its first missions. Despite this, *Hauptmann* Joseph Vollmer, chief designer in the *Kraftfahrzeug-Bereich* (motor vehicle section) at the *Kriegsministerium* (war ministry), had commenced work on a completely different successor: the A7V-U. The track now followed the rhomboid-shaped armoured superstructure, strongly resembling British practice – obviously, Vollmer must have been given the opportunity to examine, in detail, some of the many British tanks captured by German forces. However, in due course, a sole prototype was built and revealed a number of problems that were actually expected by the designer, resulting in all work being immediately cancelled.

At around the same time as the A7V-U was planned to enter service, Vollmer began work on a tank under the designation *leichter Kampfwagen* (LK – light tank) I. The most important requirement was to keep the mechanical design simple, since a tank in this weight class would be easier and more economical to produce, permitting larger numbers to be manufactured.

Vollmer found an ingeniously simple approach. He had discovered that approximately 1,000 passenger cars, with engines from 18hp to 60hp, were being stored in the depots of the *Kraftwagen-Abteilungen* (motor vehicle departments). The reason for this storage is ultimately unknown, but these vehicles were notorious among the troops, who called them '*Benzin-und Pneu-Fresser*' (petrol and tyre guzzlers). Vollmer planned to strip them and use the chassis for his new design. He utilized the frames with two additional frames added to each side, on which the suspension, comprising six bogies (the rear five were sprung), would be fitted. He also utilized the rear axle and its mountings to carry the rear drive sprockets.

The superstructure, fabricated from 14mm armour plate, protected the front-mounted 60hp Daimler four-cylinder engine, the transmission and fuel tank. The underside of the vehicle was fabricated from 8mm plate to protect mechanical parts and the crew of three: a commander, a driver and a gunner.

The LK I was armed with a 7.92mm MG 08 – some sources state two guns, but all available photographic evidence indicates otherwise – mounted in a manually operated rotatable turret on the rear section of the vehicle.

The *Leichttraktor* (LK – light tractor) 1 was based on a simple design and that made it ideal for mass production. The armoured body was mounted on the chassis frame of a civilian heavy passenger car.

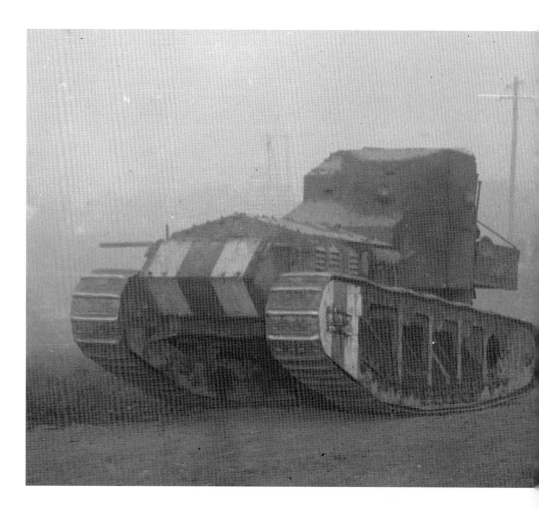

A variant mounting a 3.7cm gun was proposed with the weapon behind a fixed open-top armoured shield, known as a *Brustwehr* (parapet), that would have severely restricted side traverse.

The vehicle was fitted with an additional low-ratio gearbox to improve climbing performance and increase towing capacity. Maximum speed on paved roads was 14kph, and with the reduction gearbox engaged, it could ascend an incline of up to 41 degrees in first gear or traverse a trench up to 2m wide. However, the LK I could not operate over deeply cratered terrain churned up by heavy artillery fire.

The limited engine power of the cannibalized cars forced Vollmer to keep within certain weight limits and also led him to solve the problems of overheating engines and poor air supply.

Two prototypes had been built by mid-1918, but after extensive testing the decision was taken to cancel any planned production. In reality, the LK I was more like a tracked armoured car than a tank.

The Medium Tank Mk A 'Whippet' was designed to be a support vehicle for the slower-moving heavy tank. The type mounted four machine guns with which to attack entrenched enemy troops as the heavy tanks made the breakthrough. (NARA)

Vollmer was forced back to the drawing board and by the end of 1918 had designed an upgraded version; the LK II. Externally it was very similar to the LK I, but had much-improved engine cooling and a better system for supplying air throughout the vehicle. Furthermore, Vollmer gave serious consideration to using a turret-mounted 5.7cm Maxim-Nordenfelt rather than a 3.7cm gun. Despite series production being initiated, not one of the 24 that were completed entered front-line service: peace had finally arrived on 11 November 1918.

Although both LK types appear to resemble the British Medium Tank Mk A, known as the 'Whippet', this has to be seen as coincidental since the latter was on the battlefront in 1918, while the LK I was purely experimental and the LK II prototype was entering trials. Significantly, the hull on both German vehicles was not specifically designed to carry the suspension and running gear, nor was it fabricated from armoured steel to protect the vehicle and crew from mines and shellfire when in combat. The proposal made by Vollmer to arm the LK II with a 5.7cm gun could have resulted in a very effective armoured vehicle, but only if it had much better armour.

After the end of the war, Sweden acquired ten of these vehicles and 14 were delivered to Hungary without the knowledge of the Inter-Allied Control Commission – export documentation listed them as *Dampfkessel-Bleche* (steam boiler plates).

Next Ten Years

From 1919 to 1923, the fledgling democratic Weimar Republic continued to struggle with the consequences of the war and was making a weak attempt to consolidate a dire situation with the economy. The armed forces of the *Reichswehr*, restricted by the Treaty of Versailles, initially tried to maintain its position in the Reich. A *Generalstab* (general staff) was forbidden, prompting the establishment of a false department secretly known as the *Truppenamt* (troop office). In 1919, *Generaloberst* Hans von Seeckt, a veteran of World War I, took command of the office.

In light of the chaotic political situation in the republic, von Seeckt, assisted by the *Reichswehrminister* (secretary of defence) Otto Geßler, conceived the policy of non-partisanship for the *Reichswehr*. He was known to vehemently oppose the political left and, even more problematic, he attempted to avoid any interference by the German parliament. As a result, he can be seen as being largely responsible for the *Reichswehr* becoming a state within the state.

In 1920, von Seeckt refused to deploy the army against forces from the paramilitary *Sturmabteilung* (SA – storm division), *Der Stahlhelm* (World War I veterans) and *Freikorps* units that were staging anti-government revolts in various parts of Germany. However, he did order the *Reichswehr* to intervene when left-wing forces staged a revolt in *besetztes Ruhrgebiet* (occupied Ruhr).

His challenging relationship with German politicians is evinced by a conversation he had with *Reichspräsident* (Reich President) Friedrich Ebert. When the latter asked von Seeckt where the *Reichswehr* (Reich Defence) stood, he replied that 'the *Reichswehr* stands behind me'. Ebert then asked whether it was reliable, to which von Seeckt replied 'I do not know if it is reliable, but it does stand behind me'.

These were difficult times for the first ever democratically elected government in Germany.

The armed forces commanded by von Seeckt, secretly known as the *schwarze* (black) *Reichswehr*, began to train a new officer class in the leadership required to coordinate the infantry, artillery, armoured forces and airpower on the battlefield.

On 16 April 1922, Germany and the Soviet Union signed The Treaty of Rapallo to allow both countries to cooperate on numerous military projects in total secrecy. As a result, a *Panzerschule* (tank school) was established and codenamed 'Kama' – this was derived from the location, Kazan, and the name of the officer, *Oberstleutnant Malbrandt*, who found the site.

Kama also became the location for a *Gas-Testgelände* (gas testing site) and a highly secret *Testgelände für Chemische Waffen* (testing site for chemical weapons), code-named 'Volsk-18'. From 1925 until September 1933, a joint *Luftwaffe* and Soviet air force *Kampffliegerschule* (fighter-pilot school) operated from an airfield near the city of Lipetsk.

In 1925, *Inspektion* (In – inspectorate) 6, *Waffen und Gerat* (weapons and equipment) of the *Waffenamt* (Wa – weapons bureau), issued contracts to Daimler-Benz, Krupp and Rheinmetall-Borsig for the development of a tank in the 20,000kg class, a medium tank according to the nomenclature of the time. The contracts were fulfilled after each company had delivered two vehicles, each designated, for secrecy, as a *Großtraktor* (GrTr – heavy tractor). All were then extensively tested at a number of locations, including at Kama, but none was selected for production.

Developed in secret, the *Großtraktor* (GrTr – heavy tractor) must be considered as the first modern German tank. The type was never intended for mass production, but as a vehicle to trial the concept and test the many mechanical components.

In 1928, the same three companies were each issued with a contract for the design and development of a light tank, but German tank manufacturers had little experience to call on.

The specification issued by In.6 stipulated that the type was to be armed with a 3.7cm Rheinmetall gun mounted in a rotatable turret and have space for a crew of three or four. The type was to be capable of 40kph on the road and 20kph over rough terrain, and have a maximum weight of some 6,000kg. The specification also noted that the chassis should be designed so that it could be easily adapted for other purposes, serving alternately as a *Versorgungstracktor* (supply tractor), a *Selbstfahrlafette* (Sf – self-propelled carriage) mounting a 3.7cm *Panzerabwehrkanone* (PaK – anti-tank gun) and a *Beobachtungswagen* (BeobWg – observation tank), and also an unspecified type for civilian use.

Daimler-Benz withdrew from the contract at its own request, but Krupp and Rheinmetall continued to work in total secrecy on the vehicle spuriously designated as a *Kleintraktor* (KlTr – small tractor). However, this was soon changed to *Leichttraktor* (LTr – light tractor), since the *Waffenamt* had already begun planning the production of a smaller light tank.

The armour on the front of the LTr was to be 14mm and impervious to 13mm *Spitzgeschoss mit Kern* (SmK – armour-piercing ammunition), but only 5mm–8mm on the sides and rear, giving little protection from SmK.

The Rheinmetall-built LK was designed as a light tank and armed with a 3.7cm gun mounted in a rotatable turret. The engine and drive components were positioned in the front of the body, whereas the fuel tanks were situated on the outside behind the suspension.

It was agreed that the main armament would be a 3.7cm PaK, designed and manufactured by Rheinmetall, mounted in a rotatable turret. The same weapon was also to be issued to *Panzerabwehr* (PzAbw – anti-tank) units.

Both prototypes were very similar in appearance and, contrary to later German practice, the engine was installed in a compartment at the front of the hull with the final drive in the rear.

Both companies used different suspension methods, possibly to evaluate their practical advantages or disadvantages prior to production.

The running gear on the Krupp vehicle had four bogies, each with two double running wheels – the front and rear were of a larger diameter – and a complicated system of four encapsulated coil springs, each damping two of the bogies. The bolted-type tracks, supported by two return rollers, ran over the front idler wheel and the drive sprocket at the rear.

Rheinmetall used a much less complicated system of 12 bogies, each with two small-diameter double running wheels. Each two-bogey truck was suspended on a horizontal leaf spring. An additional running wheel between the idler wheel and the first running wheel bogey prevented the hull from grounding when climbing an obstacle. Interestingly, Rheinmetall decided to protect the entire running gear with an armoured cover.

As trials progressed, the company changed the running gear several times. At first a rubber block and steel-type lubricated track was used, since it was expected that this would result in lower ground pressure and better driving characteristics. However, these changes made the running gear more susceptible to damage, necessitating an increase in maintenance.

In 1932, the track was replaced by a conventional steel track with lubricated pins. At around the same time, the second Rheinmetall prototype underwent an extensive rebuild. The original complicated running gear was removed and replaced by four much larger double running wheels suspended on large crank-type arms, each fitted with an external coil spring. The company decided to retain the lubricated pin-type steel tracks that allowed higher speeds, although the vehicle had tendency to rock on its suspension. A similar design was used for the first prototype of the *Zugführer-Wagen* (ZW – platoon leader's vehicle), which later became the *Panzerkampfwagen* (PzKpfw – tank) III.

Basically, the visual similarity of the two LTr prototype vehicles to the numerically most important British medium tank of the time is striking. Since the development of the light tractors began some ten years earlier, it is possible that the *Waffenamt* had provided both Krupp and Rheinmetall with intelligence gathered by German field agents (spies).

Vickers Medium Mk I and Mk II

After World War I, the British military was to disband a large part of its tank force leaving only five battalions equipped with the Heavy Tank Mk V and the Medium Tank Mk C, despite the fact that both types were considered to be obsolete. The development of a successor, the Medium Tank Mk D, was a lengthy process that consumed all the allocated funding and was, ultimately, deemed a failure. This caused Colonel Philip Johnson, head of the Tank Design Department, to cancel all work on, and any planned production of, the type. The department was permanently closed in 1923.

Severe post-war financial constraints caused the British government to withdraw from the development of tanks. However, the directors of Vickers-Armstrongs Limited decided that the company would produce a tank as a private venture. In 1923, the company displayed their Light Tank Mk I, later identified as the Vickers Medium Tank Mk I.

The vehicle differed significantly in design to the British tanks in World War I by having a number of advanced mechanical features. For example, a relatively flat tracked running gear, positioned at the sides of the hull, and superstructure gave excellent road and off-road performance.

The vehicle carried a crew of five: a commander, driver, gunner, loader and mechanic.

The type was armed with an Ordnance Quick Firing (OQF) 3-Pounder (37mm) gun mounted in a large (three-man) manually rotated turret. The secondary armament was significant – four 7.7mm Hotchkiss Benét-Mercié MG in ball-type mountings and two Vickers 0.303in MG.

The vehicle was powered by a 90hp Armstrong Siddeley V8-cylinder air-cooled petrol engine, which was also used to power aircraft. The designers, conscious of the importance of weight distribution, positioned the engine to the left of the driver and placed the gearbox under the commander's position. A simple propellor shaft connected the transmission to the rear-mounted final drive unit. In action, this layout revealed many disadvantages, but it seems that ease of maintenance took precedence. Production ended after some 100 of the type had been delivered.

In 1925, the company introduced the Medium Mk II, an improved version fitted with a slightly altered superstructure, and produced some 180 vehicles. Both the Medium Mk I and Medium Mk II were issued to replace a number of the Heavy Tank Mk V that were being withdrawn from service.

The Vickers Medium was finally withdrawn from front-line service in 1938, but continued to be used by training units for developing battle tactics to be used by future tank forces.

The Vickers Medium Tank Mk II was in many ways the first modern British tank. It is obvious that this vehicle had a significant influence on the designers of the German *Kleintraktor* (KTr – small tractor).

A troop of Vickers Medium Tank Mk II leave the village of Collingbourne Ducis, Wiltshire, UK, as they return to their barracks in Warminster after a training exercise on Salisbury Plain.

Technical Comparison

LK II

Year:	1919
Weight:	7,700kg
Crew:	Three
Armament:	One MG; alternatively one 3.7cm gun
Armour:	4mm–14mm
Engine:	55hp Benz, four-cylinder, water-cooled petrol
Range (maximum):	70km
Speed (maximum):	14kph

Krupp LK II

Year:	1929
Weight:	8,700kg
Crew:	Four
Armament:	One 3.7cm KwK; one heavy MG
Armour:	5mm–14mm
Engine:	100hp Daimler M36, four-cylinder, water-cooled petrol
Range (maximum):	140km
Speed (maximum):	30kph

Rheinmetall LK II

Year:	1929
Weight:	9,000kg
Crew:	Four
Armament:	One 3.7cm KwK; one heavy MG
Armour:	5mm–14mm
Engine:	100hp Daimler M36, four-cylinder, water-cooled petrol
Range (maximum):	140km
Speed (maximum):	30kph

Vickers Medium Mk I and Mk II

Year:	1925–1934
Weight:	12,400kg
Crew:	Five
Armament:	One OQF 3-Pdr gun; four 7.7mm Hotchkiss MG; two 0.303in Vickers MG
Armour:	6mm - 8mm
Engine:	90hp Armstrong Siddeley V8, air-cooled petrol
Range (maximum):	200km
Speed (maximum):	25kph

Despite the surprising similarities, a direct comparison between the Vickers Medium Mk II and the German light tractors reveals some differences. For example, the British tank weighed 12,000kg, some 25 percent heavier.

A similar case was the German *Neubaufahrzeug* (NbFz – new build vehicle), which can be considered a further development of the GrTr. This medium tank entered service in 1935, and was strikingly similar to the Vickers Medium Mk III that was designed as a multi-turret tank and mounted an OQF 3-Pdr gun in the main turret with two smaller MG-armed turrets mounted parallel to the driver.

The NbFz had a similar layout, but interestingly carried two powerful guns in the main turret – a 7.5cm *Kampfwagenkanone* (KwK – tank gun) and a 3.7cm KwK. Two secondary turrets, each mounting an MG 34, were fitted to the right and rear left in front of the main turret.

Both the Vickers Medium Mk III and the NbFz were not intended for mass production, but instead were treated as valuable proof of concept vehicles.

As for the ongoing development of a medium tank, both Great Britain and the German Reich continued to develop what each considered to be the ideal vehicle.

The *Neubaufahrzeug* (NbFz – new build vehicle) followed models being produced in a number of countries. Designed as a multi-turret tank, it carried a crew of six and mounted a 7.5cm KwK 37 multi-purpose cannon, a 3.7cm KwK 36 anti-tank gun and a 7.92mm MG 34 in the main turret. An MG 34 was installed in each of the two side turrets.

Rearmament 2

After the end of World War I, Germany had no option other than to sign the Treaty of Versailles in January 1920. The document held Germany solely responsible for the outbreak of the war and detailed far-reaching conditions that included the cessation of territory, reparations to the victorious powers and extensive disarmament.

The military stipulations included:

- The dissolution of the Grand General Staff
- The probation of compulsory military service
- The capping of the professional army at a maximum of 4,000 officers and 100,000 men
- The capping of the navy at a maximum of 15,000 men, six heavy (armoured) cruisers, six cruisers, 12 destroyers and 12 torpedo boats
- A ban on heavy weapons such as battleships, submarines and tanks
- A ban on the development and production of chemical and gas warfare agents
- A ban on the re-establishment of an air force
- A ban on the building of fortifications along any German border

Germany had not been involved in the drafting of the treaty document, a fact that left a majority of the population feeling that the very harsh conditions it contained were not only unjust, but also humiliating. This resentment grew over the following 12 years and the German people became convinced that a dictatorship would provide salvation. In 1933, Adolf Hitler and his *Nationalsozialistische Deutsche Arbeiterpartie* (NSDAP – National Socialist German Worker's Party), came to power on the premise of being able to rebuild a great and powerful *Vaterland* (Fatherland).

Opposite: The Treaty of Versailles prevented Germany from posessing or producing tanks. Here *Reichswehr* tank crewmen lift a *Kampfwagen Nachbildung* (dummy combat vehicle). It was assembled from three components, fabricated from wood and canvas, to replicate the shape of a light tank and then fitted over the chassis of a commercially available car – here a BMW Dixi.

Germany had already managed to secretly circumvent many of the conditions set out in the treaty despite all activities being closely monitored by allied observers.

The sale of armaments to other countries, especially any work associated with tanks, was closely scrutinized. Officials and employees in the foreign missions of the *Reichswehr*, were actively encouraged to gather information by any means, including espionage, and private citizens were also supposed to get involved.

In 1926, Munich-based publisher J. F. Lehmann produced *Heigl's Taschenbuch der Tanks* (Pocket Book of Tanks) by Fritz Heigl, a *Waffentechniker* (weapon technician [specialist]) who taught at the *Technische Hochschule* (technical college) in Vienna. His book was a study of tank development in countries around the world. The publication was considered to be an important source of information to many, including German military planners. Heigl continued to update his book until his death in 1930.

The then Major Heinz Guderian, who is regarded as the progenitor of the *Panzerwaffe*, was commander of the *Truppenamt für Heerestransport* (troop office for army transport) in 1927. He also worked there as a tactical instructor and this made it possible for him to visit military units in other countries to observe training exercises and examine the latest armoured and transport vehicles. In 1929, he visited the barracks of the *Livregementets husarer* (Life Regiment Hussars) in Skövde, Sweden, as a member of a military

Three of the ten German-built LK II secretly purchased by Sweden in contravention of the Treaty of Versailles by using false export documentation in which they were listed as 'boiler plating'. The type entered service as the *Stridsvagn* (Strv – tank) m/21 and was armed with an Austrian-manufactured 6.5mm Schwarzlose machine gun. (Swedish Army Museum)

delegation and it was there that he was to ride on a tank for the first time. It is not without irony that this vehicle, the *Stridsvagn* (Strv – tank) m/21, had been developed in Germany at the end of World War I as the LK II.

A First Mass Tank

While the first German post-war GrTr and KlTr tanks were still being tested at Kama, the *Heereswaffenamt* (HWa – army ordnance office) initiated the development of another light tank. The German requirements were similar to those of other countries – create an easily manufactured tank that could be produced economically and perform various tactical tasks. Apparently, this design was required urgently.

From the minutes of a meeting held at the HWa on 14 February 1930:

> The head of the HWa has already suggested the development of a *Kleinpanzer* [KlPz – small tank] during his visit to *Heeresversuchsstelle* [HV – army testing site] Kummersdorf. The specification for its use as a reconnaissance vehicle, weapons carrier or a light tractor is still being worked on. Whether such a small tank could be used in a battle is highly debatable. For this reason, a new set of drawings have to be produced (including those for an armoured reconnaissance vehicle), since those currently available are misleading. We recommend the purchase of a Carden-Loyd Tankette, to avoid many years of unnecessary, time-consuming development.

Future Royal Armoured Corps (RAC) tank drivers undergoing instruction in the Carden-Loyd Tankette Mk IV. The British companies Vickers and Carden-Loyd did valuable, pioneering work in the field of tank technology in the 1920s. (Getty)

Carden-Loyd

Founded in 1924 by Sir John Carden and Vivian Loyd, Carden-Loyd Tractors Limited went on to have a significant influence on the development of the light tank.

Their first design incorporated the ideas of a British officer, Major Giffard le Quesne Martel, and resulted in their One-man Tankette produced in 1925. By 1927, the Carden-Loyd tankette was ready for production and was subsequently exported worldwide.

The mechanical design was kept very simple by utilizing readily available components – a 23hp water-cooled, four-cylinder engine from the Ford Model T – was used to power the vehicle and the gearbox came from a readily available commercial vehicle. The tankette was fitted with simple link and pin track that ran over 11 small unsprung steel rollers mounted between two guide rails and fitted with simple shock absorbers. The vehicle was steered by differential braking – the left-hand brake would be applied to turn left.

Carden-Loyd also introduced the concept of modular construction to the tank industry. Instead of designing tanks as an entirety, the company developed components that could be easily replaced or modified. This allowed the armed forces to efficiently modernize their tanks without having to replace complete vehicles, an approach that was later adopted by many other manufacturers and influenced future tank development.

The hull and fighting compartment on a Carden-Loyd Tankette was fabricated from 6mm and 9mm plates. For simplicity, the top of the fighting compartment was left open, leaving the driver and gunner, who fired the 0.303in Vickers water-cooled machine gun, vulnerable to the weather, infantry fire and shrapnel (shell fragments).

In March 1928, the engineering company Vickers-Armstrongs Limited purchased Carden-Loyd Tractors Limited.

Vickers Carden-Loyd continued to develop the tankette and almost immediately began making improvements by installing a 40hp Ford Model A engine and fitting a significantly improved track and running gear. Production finally ended in 1935

Carden-Loyd tankettes had a great influence on the development of military tactics to be employed by the British Army. Many military exercises were held to identify the strengths or expose any weaknesses of the type under battlefield conditions, and the resultant findings would then be carefully evaluated for use in the development of later tanks.

This Vickers Light Tank Mk II carries a British civilian licence plate, indicating that it is one of the many pre-production vehicles built. Note it is fitted with non-standard running gear.

The then *Generalfeldmarschall*, Hermann Göring, accompanied by officers from the *Luftwaffe*, inspect a Carden-Loyd Tankette after the annexation of Czech-Sudetenland. The type had inadequate armour and was poorly armed with a single machine gun.

In 1930, the Vickers Carden-Loyd Tankette began to attract foreign interest and some ten countries were to buy, usually in small numbers, the Mk VI version. More important was that Vickers-Armstrongs decided to allow other companies to produce the type under licence. Many of these carried out a thorough mechanical evaluation before modifying the type to their own specification and readying it for production. The Soviet Union alone manufactured more than 3,000 of these vehicles as the T-27, while France produced the Renault *Chenillette* [caterpillar] UE. The tankette was also manufactured in Poland, Japan, Italy and Czechoslovakia.

In service, the tracked vehicle proved to be more versatile for towing, especially in heavy mud, than a conventional wheeled type. This was noted by the manufacturer and they immediately initiated the design of what became the Vickers Carden-Loyd Tractor in 1930.

The vehicle was powered by a Meadows EPC six-cylinder, water-cooled petrol engine, that was installed, slightly offset to the right, directly behind the driver. The hull was widened and fitted with completely redesigned running gear with four bogies, each with two leaf-sprung rollers. A wider track was fitted which significantly improved service life.

Now that the chassis finally had the required stability, the British Army became much more interested in the vehicle. After further improvements, which included fitting a Horstmann-type coil suspension to replace the original leaf-spring type, the vehicle was approved as ready for service.

The same chassis was also utilized as the basis for a number of light tanks. The most important of these was the Vickers Light Tank Mk VI, which was produced in large numbers for the British Army and remained in front-line service, as the backbone of their reconnaissance units, until 1942.

The British Army used various light tanks manufactured by Vickers. The most important type was the Light Tank Mk VI, which was used in the colonies and then for reconnaissance in North Africa until it was replaced by the US-supplied M3 (Stuart Mk I to Mk V).

Kleintraktor

The Carden-Loyd Tractor purchased by the HWa was thoroughly examined by engineers who found that it, more or less, met their expectations by being mechanically sound and having acceptable performance.

A series of test drives showed that the track when driven by the front sprocket performed surprisingly well. All previous German tank designs had rear drive that had a tendency to throw a track when violent steering movements were made – this frequently occurred with the LTr when the type was undergoing trials at Kama, but despite modifications made by designers and engineers, the problem had remained unsolved.

Krupp finally delivered a first prototype in 1932, which for secrecy was identified as the *Kleintraktor* (KlTr – small tractor). The vehicle was essentially a copy of the Carden-Loyd Tractor, except that the running gear had an extra running wheel and the two rear roller carriages were connected by a stabilizing bar. Unlike the Carden-Loyd running gear, the track was guided at the top by two return rollers. The machine was powered by a 3,500cc Krupp M 301 six-cylinder, boxer-type (horizontally opposed cylinders) air-cooled engine that was mounted centrally at the rear. Later prototypes were fitted with the more powerful M 305, which boasted 60hp.

The transmission remained in the front and was connected to the engine by a Cardan-type shaft (with a universal joint at each end); a configuration that became standard for all future German tanks.

Germany acquired a Vickers Carden-Loyd Tractor in 1931. The vehicle was comprehensively examined and extensively tested. The chassis was then used as a template for the German *Kleintraktor* (KlTr – small tractor), which eventually became the PzKpfw I.

After several pre-production vehicles had been built had delivered for trials, the PzKpfw I Ausf A entered production at the beginning of 1935. Note the vehicle has been finished in standard *Buntfarben-Anstrich* (three-tone camouflage), but carries no other markings.

Early trials at Kama showed that the KlTr had good driving and steering characteristics. The trials were continued at HV Kummersdorf and included comparative drives with the Carden-Loyd Tractor.

According to a test report, the KlTr clearly outperformed its British 'competitor' in all essential aspects, including driving characteristics. Sharp turns could be made without a track being thrown and many drivers commented on the vehicle having a smooth gear shift and a mechanically reliable transmission. The trials also indicated that the tracks had a service life of some 4,000km; considerably more than the 2,700km Carden-Loyd claimed their vehicle could achieve.

As a result of the trials, the HWa was sufficiently confident to issue a contract to build six of the type.

PzKpfw I

As the development of the KlTr continued, the HWa initiated a series of meetings to discuss the role of the type on the battlefield.

One of their first considerations was to produce an effective combat vehicle by installing a 2cm cannon. Officials decided that the weapon was to be mounted in an open superstructure, although this would limit traverse.

However, the HWa eventually decided not to equip the KlTr with this weapon, and all planning for a '2cm tank' was shelved. It is possible that German engineers found that there was insufficient space in the vehicle to mount the gun and also that Rheinmetall had not begun producing the weapon.

From 1935 onwards, the new light tanks were used in many manoeuvres for crews to gain both mechanical and tactical experience. Here, field engineers examine the Krupp M 305 boxer-type engine.

As a result, the HWa decided that the vehicle was to be armed with two 7.92mm machine guns. Subsequently, Krupp received a contract for the design and development of an armoured superstructure and a one-man rotatable turret.

In 1934, the *Deutsche Reichswehrministerium* (German Imperial Defence Ministry) ordered that development of the new tank was to be given top priority under the secret designation *Landwirtschaftlicher Schlepper* (LaS – agricultural tractor). The build-up of the *Wehrmacht* had begun and would continue, backed by the might of German heavy industry.

On 6 March 1935, a statement made by Hermann Göring – that 'a German army of 400,000 men was insufficient' – heralded the beginning of a massive rearmament programme.

A few months later, the HWa redesignated the LaS as the PzKpfw I. The light tank was to be mass produced by Krupp and have a combat weight of 5,400kg. The hull and superstructure were fabricated from sheet *Panzerstahl* (rolled steel) which had a maximum thickness of 13mm. The fighting compartment was very narrow, resulting in the turret being positioned to the right of the centre line. The PzKpfw I was armed with two 7.92mm MG 13k machine guns, each fitted with a 25-round *Stangenmagazin* (bar magazine) – this weapon would be discontinued in 1936 and replaced by the 7.92mm MG 34, which was to become the standard issue for all German forces.

Left: The PzKpfw I carried a crew of two, a driver and the commander, who also had to operate the two MG 13k. It was standard practice to remove the weapons when vehicles were in the workshop area of their home garrison.

Below: Due to a lack of more suitable vehicles, the *Reichswehr* was forced to continue using the Krupp-built LK for a lengthy period of tactical exercises. This LK is fitted with a frame antenna for Morse code communications.

Nuremberg, 1936:
The latest tanks played
an important role in
German propaganda.
Here, a column of
PzKpfw I parade through
a Swastika-bedecked
stadium during one of
the many *Reichsparteitag*
(Nazi Party) rallies.
(Getty)

A test vehicle showing the effect of a simulated close hit by a 50kg bomb. The superstructure is intact and only shows superficial damage from shrapnel.

The installation of a 3,460cc Krupp M 305 air-cooled engine was criticized from the beginning of production simply because of its poor power-to-weight ratio. As a result, the HWa issued contracts to a number of manufacturers for the design of a more powerful engine. Eventually, Maybach delivered their 3,790cc NL 38 TR six-cylinder water-cooled petrol engine and was subsequently awarded a production contract. However, the Maybach engine required an efficient cooling system and this necessitated a much larger engine bay. Consequently, engineers at Krupp decided that the only solution was to lengthen the hull by some 40cm and change the running gear by fitting an extra roller and a larger-diameter idler wheel at the rear. Otherwise, the vehicle remained virtually unchanged.

Although the new vehicle was designated as the PzKpfw I *Ausführung* (Ausf – mark or model) B, the first production tanks were, for an unknown reason, classified as the Ausf A.

As the build-up of the German tank force continued at pace, so did the adoption of new operational tactics that were primarily based on the theoretical work of Oswald Lutz and Heinz Guderian in the 1920s. Since there were

almost no tanks available, as an expedient, future tank commanders and crews 'fought' battles using *Attrappen* (dummy tanks). At first these had a tubular metal chassis with bicycle wheels and a tank-like superstructure constructed from canvas and wood. Later, this same type of superstructure would be fitted over a civilian light car, such as a BMW Dixi. Tactical exercises using dummy tanks continued until 1933/34, when a number of LaS were delivered.

The final stage of driver training would be conducted in a production PzKpfw I over a combat training area.

Both Lutz and Guderian had realized that for their combat tactics to be truly effective, a reliable means of communication was essential to allow battle orders to be received by the rapidly advancing tanks. Although it is known that the HWa issued an order for all tanks to be prepared ready for the installation of radio equipment, it is not known when this became available in sufficient quantities. Photographs taken during the first exercises show tank commanders using signal flags, which possibly indicates a lack of radio equipment.

The standard radio equipment installed in the PzKpfw I Ausf A and PzKpfw I Ausf B was an *Ultrakurzwellen* (Ukw – ultra-short wave [VHF]) *Funkgerät* (Fu – radio device) 2 and an *Empfänger* (E – receiver) c1 fitted with a converter, but these only allowed a commander to receive messages.

Right: Two PzKpfw I Ausf A pass a 7.5cm le FH 16 during a large-scale exercise held in the late 1930s. The engine hatches on both tanks have been opened to improve ventilation for the Krupp M 305 air-cooled engine.

Right: Driver training: When negotiating a steep slope, a driver had to operate the brakes to control speed, causing his tank to tip, briefly placing a heavy load on the *Seitenvorelage* (final drive units).

Below: The command tank was developed in parallel with the establishment of the tank units. The kl PzBefWg (SdKfz 265) was the first to be produced and utilized a PzKpfw I Ausf B chassis. The large frame antenna was fitted to increase radio range.

Above: The development of the PzKpfw II began in 1935. Here, a test chassis is being driven across a temporary bridge.

Right: The ability to climb over an obstacle, such as a wall or defensive rampart, or cross trenches was a very important important factor. Here, a PzKpfw I climbs an earth bank topped with a vertical barricade.

Above: The Wriezen/ Oder *Panzerschule* (tank school) in 1943: Both the PzKpfw I Ausf A and PzKpfw I Ausf B were issued to tank driving schools.

Left: The driver's position in what trainees called a *Fahrschulwanne* (driver school tub). The instrument panel, steering levers and gear-change are clearly visible.

Training Vehicle

Private car ownership was somewhat rare in Germany at the beginning of the 1930s, and although light cars were readily available, most were too expensive for a working citizen. There were plans for an inexpensive *volkswagen* (people's car), but only a very small number had been manufactured by 1939. Consequently, the people of Germany, unlike those of the US, had little or no experience of driving a motor vehicle. Senior commanders of the fledgling *Wehrmacht* were alarmed and issued an order for driver training to be given the highest priority.

The first 150 LaS were completed as chassis only vehicles (the engine compartment was protected by a box-like cover) and issued to newly formed *Panzerfahrschule* (tank driver school).

In the period before a combat-ready PzKpfw I became available, these basic LaS vehicles were also used in the first unit-size exercises held to practise battlefield tactics. Soon after the PzKpfw I Ausf B entered service, a large number were completed as driver training vehicles. The type was very similar to the earlier LaS, but was fitted with a safety railing around the seating area to protect the student and his driving instructor.

Although the frame antenna on a PzBefWg tank significantly improved radio transmission range, it made the vehicle easy for enemy gunners to identify. But military planners had become aware of this and, from 1942, all command vehicles were fitted with a less conspicuous *Sternantenne* (star antenna) 'd'.

In 1938, it was decided that the commander of each light tank company should be issued with a kl PzBefWg. Those built on the Pzkpfw I Ausf B chassis vehicle had a larger superstructure to accommodate a radio operator.

Right: The first kl PzBefWg were built on chassis of the PzKpfw I Ausf A, but production stopped after 15 had been delivered.

Below: When the PzKpfw I and PzKpfw II entered front-line service, both were equipped with a radio a receiver, whereas the kl PzBefWg had a transmitter.

These vehicles were of great value, allowing thousands of tank drivers to be trained effectively and realistically for the later successes achieved by the *Panzerwaffe*.

Despite all its efforts, German heavy industry was never able to supply the *Panzerwaffe* with an adequate number of armoured vehicles. This problem did not only affect those on the battlefront, but also those training divisions first established in 1939. In particular, the 16 *Panzer-Ersatz-Abteilungen* (PzErsAbt – tank replacement battalions), although vital to the war effort, were constantly short of vehicles. Consequently, all of the PzKpfw I Ausf A and PzKpfw I Ausf B training vehicles produced had to remain in service until the end of the war.

Command Tank

Military planners were aware that to ensure tactical command as the battle progressed, a dedicated vehicle, fitted with a powerful radio, must be developed. In 1935, a command version of the PzKpfw I Ausf A was produced with a distinctive wide and turretless box-shaped superstructure The type was fitted with a 20W S c and a E c1 (Fu 6).

The kl PzBefWg Ausf B tank carried a ball-mounted 7.92mm MG 34 for self-defence.

PzKpfw I Ausf A

Year:	1933–1935
Weight:	5,400kg
Crew:	Two
Weapons:	Two 7.92mm MG 13k
Radio:	Fu 2 E
Armour:	13mm
Engine:	3,460cc Krupp M 305, air-cooled, petrol
Range (maximum):	140km
Speed (maximum):	40kph

PzKpfw I Ausf B

Year:	1935–1939
Weight:	5,800kg
Crew:	Two
Weapons:	Two 7.92mm MG 13k or standard MG 13
Radio:	Fu 2 E
Armour:	13mm
Engine:	3,790cc Maybach NL 35 TR, six-cylinder, water-cooled, petrol
Range (maximum):	170km
Speed (maximum):	40kph

Note: NL (*Normalleistungsmotor* – normal [standard] performance engine)
      TR (*Trockensumpfschmierung* – dry sump lubrication)

Rheinmetall LK II

Year:	1929
Weight:	9,000kg
Crew:	Four
Armament:	3.7cm KwK, one heavy MG
Armour:	5mm to 14mm
Engine:	100hp Daimler M36, four-cylinder, water-cooled petrol
Range (maximum):	140km
Speed (maximum):	30kph

The vehicle was manned by a driver and a company commander who also operated the radio. The superstructure was fitted with three vision devices that allowed the commander to have a somewhat restricted view of the battlefield. In 1935, the first 15 vehicles were delivered and most were issued to the commanders of Panzer companies. Spare vehicles were issued to the battalion, regimental, brigade and divisional staffs of the first experimental PzDiv. The type was used for the first time during a large tactical exercise held near Münster during autumn 1935. At company level, the simple vehicle performed well as an efficient interface to those tanks equipped with a radio receiver.

The formation of 1.PzDiv, 2.PzDiv and 3.PzDiv began and continued until the end of 1935, but 4.PzDiv and 5.PzDiv would not be formed until 1938.

A simple ferry, assembled by field engineers from three standard pontoons and bridging sections, is being used to transport a PzKpfw I Ausf A across a river during a pre-war combat exercise.

As production of the PzKpfw I Ausf B increased, more chassis with which to build command tanks became available. The new type had a completely redesigned superstructure that allowed the fighting compartment to be considerably enlarged, making room for an additional crew member: a radio operator. Freed from his radio duties, the company commander could now concentrate on the battlefield, and the extra space also allowed more radio equipment to be fitted.

The command vehicles were designated *kleiner Panzerbefehlswagen* (kl PzBefWg – small armoured command vehicle) and given the identifier *Sonderkraftfahrzeug* (SdKfz – special purpose vehicle) 265.

During the build-up of the *Panzertruppe*, various attempts were made to increase the range of the radio equipment. Large frame-type antennas of various

shapes were mounted above the superstructure to improve transmitting power. Standard PzKpfw I tanks are also known to have been fitted with similar antennas, but it is not known whether this was intended to improve the signal for the Fu 2 receiver.

At company level, there was no longer a requirement for a dedicated command tank, which resulted in all SdKfz 265 being transferred to signal companies on all divisional levels.

In 1938, the *große Panzerbefehlswagen* (gr PzBefWg – large armoured command vehicle), based on the PzKpfw III, began to be issued to front-line units. The vehicle was equipped with standard Fu 6 equipment, but also carried the Fu 8 long-range medium wave transmitter. This created a closed and effective radio network within a PzDiv and its many sub-units.

The PzKpfw I Ausf B was fitted with a Maybach NL 38 TR engine. The type was longer than a Krupp 305, making it necessary to lengthen the hull and fit a fifth running wheel.

A 2cm Tank

The *Oberkommando der Heeres* (OKH – high command of the army) had, from the very beginning, planned to equip all future PzDiv with much better-armed tanks. The actual weapons were already available: a 3.7cm KwK L/45, intended to engage enemy tanks, and the 7.5cm KwK L/24, a dedicated support gun capable of destroying fortified positions, anti-tank guns and artillery. These weapons had already been extensively tested in the LTr and GrTr trials.

In 1932, another test model followed. Designed as a multi-turret tank and weighing some 23,000kg, the NbFz was classified as a medium tank. The main turret mounted a 7.5cm KwK and a 3.7cm PaK gun, and the two auxiliary turrets each mounted a 7.92mm machine gun. The type was operated by a crew of seven. Five experimental vehicles were built, but this tank was to

have no direct influence on further developments in Germany, and no orders were issued for series production. Instead, the HWa decided to introduce two different types of tank to fulfil different tasks.

The *Zugführerwagen* (ZW – platoon leader's vehicle), later the PzKpfw III, mounted a 3.7cm KwK L/45 for tank-versus-tank combat. This weapon had already been selected to equip German anti-tank units. The second type was a *Begleitwagen* (BW – escort tank) armed with a 7.5cm KwK L/24, which later became known as the PzKpfw IV.

In 1934, it became obvious to those responsible that the introduction of the ZW and BW into service would not be possible within the planned time frame – the formation of the first three Panzer divisions, although being given the highest priority, would not be completed until 1935. Consequently, military planners decided to order the development of another type of light

The PzKpfw I could cross a water obstacle up to 60cm deep. Drivers practised this action extensively, since any water entering the engine compartment could immobilize the tank.

Below: The first pre-series of PzKpfw II was developed from the LaS 100 and had a chassis fitted with three double bogies carrying a six-wheel running gear.

Left: Nuremberg, September 1938: PzKpfw II being used to demonstrate an attack on infantry positions during the final *Reichsparteitag,* which was attended by some 500,000 German citizens. (Getty)

Left: A test chassis of the PzKpfw II Ausf D. The type was designed to be a fast combat vehicle and was fitted with a Christie-type torsion bar running gear.

PzKpfw II Ausf c

Year:	1935–1939
Weight:	8,900kg
Crew:	Three
Weaponry:	One 2cm KwK 30; one 7.92mm MG 34
Radio:	Fu 5
Armour:	14.5mm, later reinforced with additional 20mm plates
Engine:	6,190cc Maybach HL 62 TR
Range (maximum):	190km
Speed (maximum):	40kph

tank. Three companies, Maschinenfabrik-Augsburg Nürmburg (MAN), Krupp and Henschel, were issued with a contract to design and develop the type designated, for secrecy, as LaS 100.

Using experience gained with the KlTr and later the PzKpfw I, MAN delivered the first trial vehicles in February 1935. The hull was slightly larger and the running gear was similar to that on the PzKpfw I Ausf B, but had six, instead of five, running wheels – two of which were mounted on leaf-sprung bogies.

The vehicle was powered by a 5,960cc Maybach HL 57 TR engine that had 100hp – hence the designation LaS 100. The type carried a crew of three and was armed with a 2cm KwK 30 and an MG 34 mounted in a rotatable turret. The tank differed from earlier types by having space in the rear left of the fighting compartment for a radioman to operate a Fu 5.

The hull, superstructure and turret were fabricated from 14.5mm armour that only gave protection from 7.92mm armour-piercing infantry ammunition.

In 1936, MAN was contracted to build three 25-vehicle, pre-production batches: the PzKpfw II Ausf a/1, PzKpfw II Ausf a/2 and PzKpfw II Ausf a/3. This was followed by a batch of 100 PzKpfw II Ausf b.

The final batch of PzKpfw II Ausf c was completed in 1938. This variant was fitted with the running gear – five large running wheels, each fitted with a leaf spring – that was to be used on future variants (except the PzKpfw II Ausf D). The PzKpfw Ausf c was fitted with a more powerful 6,190cc Maybach HL 62 TR engine to improve performance.

After the delivery of the pre-production vehicles, the PzKpfw II Ausf A (210 built) followed, then the PzKpfw II Ausf B (384 built) and the PzKpfw II Ausf C (364 built). The variants differed only in a few details, since any modification would be incorporated on the production line.

PzKpfw II Ausf D

Even before the war began, the PzKpfw II was being heavily criticized by those in the military. As a result, Major Olbrich, a technical officer in the HWa, was ordered to prepare a detailed assessment of the type.

The following points have been extracted from his notes:

> The diameter of the running wheels is far too small, and this causes excessive wear to their rubber tyres, which fail frequently.
> On the Ausf C, the external leaf springs have a service life of only 1,500km–2,500km.
> I consider the track to be far too narrow and think it should be replaced by a wider type.
> The internal layout of the hull is poor, particularly because the fuel tank is installed in the fighting compartment and must be considered to be fire hazard. The seat for the radio operator, squeezed into the rear left corner, is far too cramped.
> Field engineers have complained of the lack of access to the engine and ancillaries. The solution is to redesign the engine compartment.

In 1938, the newly formed le PzDiv began to be issued with the PzKpfw II Ausf D. Each units had a dedicated transport company equipped with Faun L 900 heavy trucks and SdAnh 115 trailers.

In 1937, Krupp offered the HWa a new engine for the PzKpfw II, but the installation of this power unit made it necessary to fundamentally redesign the hull. MAN, as the main manufacturer of the type, took up these suggestions and produced the PzKpfw II Ausf D.

For an unknown reason, the Krupp engine was never used and MAN decided to improve performance by fitting a 6,190cc Maybach HL 62 TRM. The redesign of the hull allowed the fuel tank to be positioned in an enlarged engine compartment. The radio operator, and his equipment, was repositioned to the front, on the right of the driver.

Another major change was that the vehicle now had Christie-type torsion bar suspension with five large-diameter running wheels and slightly wider tracks. The PzKpfw II Ausf D (and Ausf E) had a road speed of 55kph, but their cross-country speed was less impressive.

The first 50 of the type were selected for a special use and issued to the so-called *leichte Divisionen* (le Div – light divisions).

PzKpfw II Ausf D

Year:	1935–1939
Weight:	11,000kg
Crew:	Two or three
Weapons:	One 2cm KwK 30; one 7.92mm MG 34
Radio:	Fu 5
Armour:	30mm
Engine:	6,190cc Maybach HL 62 TRM
Range (maximum):	200km
Speed (maximum):	55kph

Note: HL (*Hockleistungmotor* – high-performance engine)
TRM (*Trockensumpfschmierung mit Magnetschnapperzündung* – dry sump lubrication with magneto ignition)

Light Tanks and the *Panzewaffe*

When Lutz and Guderian, the creators of the *Panzerwaffe*, attended the first mass exercises organized by the *Reichswehr* to work out the appropriate combat tactics, there were practically no suitable armoured vehicles available. The few that were included the heavy *Sonderwagen* (special vehicle) known as a 'SchuPo', which was purposely built for the *Schützpolizei* (security police). Another type was the *gepanzerter Kraftwagen* (armoured motor vehicle), a very basic armoured personnel carrier.

Some of the still-extant LTr and GrTr experimental vehicles tested at Kama were also used. At least one LTr had been converted into a *Führer-Panzerwagen* (command tank) with radio equipment, possibly the same as that used in the PzKpfw-based kl PzBefWg.

With the availability of the small tractors and then the PzKpfw I, the practive of using wood and canvas dummy tanks ended.

The first three PzDiv were initially to be equipped with only the PzKpfw I. These large units already demonstrated a forward-looking and very effective structure. The basic PzDiv was organized as a *Panzerbrigade* (PzBrig – tank brigade), formed from two *Panzerregimenter* (PzRgt – tank regiments) each with two *Panzer Abteilung* (PzAbt – tank battalions). Each of these four PzAbt was to have three *leichter Panzerkompanien* (le PzKp – light tank companies) and one *schwere Panzerkompanie* (s PzKp – heavy tank company).

The combat strength of the emerging armoured divisions was mainly based on the planned 3.7cm and 7.5cm-armed combat vehicles. At the beginning of 1935,

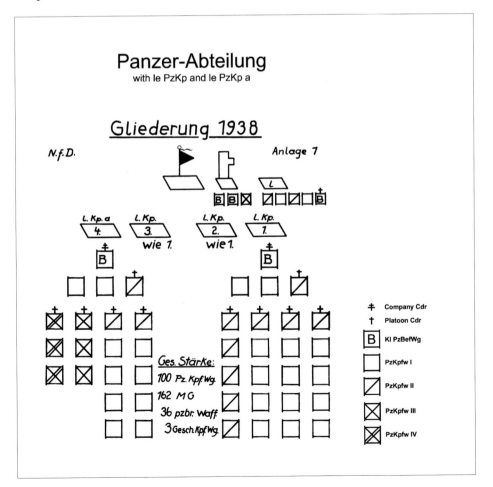

Structure of a PzDivi in 1938.

Up until 1940, a PzDiv had a complement of two PzRgt, each with two *Panzer-Abteilungen* (PzAbt – tank battalions).

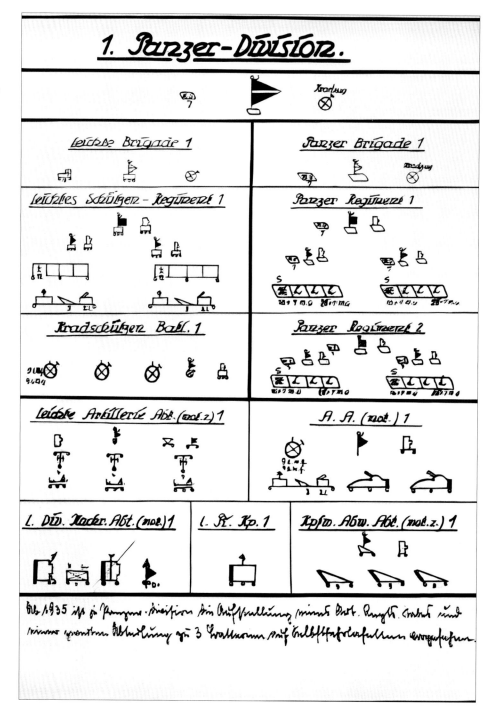

the HWa was still expecting an early delivery of these medium tanks, but this ambitious plan was altered to have 140 PzKpfw III and ten PzKpfw IV available by April 1937. However, it was not possible to keep to this schedule, since

B e i l a g e 1 zu O.K.H. AHA/Jn 6
(IVa) Nr.206/37 g.Kdos.

Zur Darstellung stärkerer Pz.Kpf.Wg. durch
schwächere sind um den Turm der letzteren farbige
Ringe nach den folgenden Mustern anzubringen:

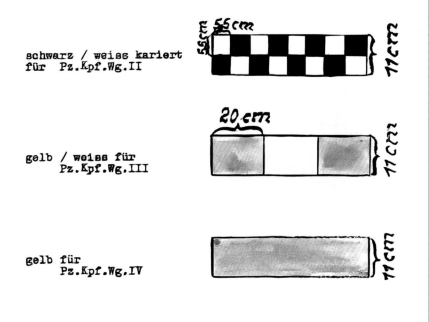

schwarz / weiss kariert
für Pz.Kpf.Wg.II

gelb / weiss für
Pz.Kpf.Wg.III

gelb für
Pz.Kpf.Wg.IV

Due to the delayed production of the PzKpfw III and PzKpfw IV, both types had to be represented by the PzKpfw I during exercises. The tanks were painted with coloured markings around the top edge of the turret to represent each type.

neither Daimler-Benz nor Krupp had completed the development of the vehicles. The missing PzKpfw III and PzKpfw VI in the companies were initially covered by PzKpfw I, and then PzKpfw II from the summer of 1937.

On 30 April 1937, the *Panzertruppe* had some 100 PzKpfw II, in addition to 1,400 PzKpfw I in service, when the OKH issued the following order:

The PzKpfw II (2cm) to be delivered are primarily to be organized in such a way that the radio equipment required for command and communications is available down to *Zug* [Zg – platoon] leader level. It must be accepted that 1.Zg to 3.Zg in the le PzKp are to have only one PzKpfw II each. The majority of available PzKpfw II are to be assigned to the 4.Zg, and are to be used in place of the missing PzKpfw III (3.7cm). This ensures that all platoon commanders are equipped with transmitters.

PzBrig 1 (1.PzDiv) will initially be issued with PzKpfw III (2cm) in such a way that it will probably be possible to arrange these platoons, the light tank platoons and light tank companies in terms of number and tank type.

This arrangement corresponds to the recent *Kriegsstärkenachweisugen* [KStN – table of organization], dated 1 October 1937. The PzKpfw and PzBefWg (command tanks) in each unit will be equipped as follows:

Kl PzBefWg
A transmitter and two receivers

PzKpfw II (2cm) when used as a command vehicle
A transmitter and a receiver

PzKpfw III (3.7cm) for company commanders and signals platoons
A transmitter and two receivers
Others
A transmitter and a receiver

PzKpfw IV (7.5cm) for company commanders and signals platoons
A transmitter and two receivers
Others
A transmitter and a receiver

All other PzKpfw
A receiver

If PzKpfw I (MG) are used to represent PzKpfw II (2cm), PzKpfw III (3.7cm) or PzKpfw IV (7.5cm), gun fire is to be simulated by firing flare cartridges from a signal pistol.

Tactical principles for the use of the PzKpfw I, PzKpfw II, PzKpfw III and PzKpfw IV:

The PzKpfw I fight against infantry targets with the two machine guns.

The PzKpfw II (2cm) shall also fight similar targets with the MG, and use the 2cm KwK against enemy tanks, other armoured vehicles and reinforced positions.

The PzKpfw III (3.7cm) with three MG is very effective against infantry. The 3.7cm KwK is a more effective against an enemy tank than a 2cm KwK. Within a current light tank company, the PzKpfw III provides very effective support in combat for the PzKpfw I and PzKpfw II, which are primarily deployed to eliminate enemy infantry. Here the well-armoured PzKpfw III gives us the advantage. The PzKpfw IV (7.5cm) is designed as a support weapon with which to eliminate important targets and provide cover as an attack progresses.

This order seems to show the precarious situation of the armoured forces in 1937. In addition to the planned tanks, there was also a serious lack of radio equipment. It was not until the beginning of the French campaign that the majority of PzKpfw III and PzKpfw IV were equipped with a transmitter and two receivers. The light types had, partly for reasons of space, less effective equipment – the PzKpfw II had a transmitter and a receiver, whereas the PzKpfw I had a receiver only. The kl PzBefWg (SdKfz 265) carried the same radio equipment as that fitted in medium tanks. In September 1939, the SdKfz 267 command vehicle entered service and was fitted with long-range medium wave transmitters.

A PzKpfw II Ausf D of PzAbt (verl) 66 being loaded on a heavy truck. The front bogie and load bed of an SdAnh 115 is being utilized as a ramp.

The rear four running wheels on the PzKpfw I had leaf springs and were stabilized by a steel beam. Only the first wheel was fitted with a coil spring.

The Light Divisions

In addition to being equipped with tanks, all PzDiv were formed with a significant infantry brigade and sub-units to consolidate any positions gained after the armoured force had achieved a breakthrough on the battlefront.

The deployment of an entire PzDiv to a distant battlefront could only be achieved by using rail transport. Although effective, such an operation consumed valuable time to organize followed by the loading and unloading of tanks, vehicles and ancillary equipment.

In order to make armoured units more quickly available in critical situations, the concept of the *leichte Division* (le Div – light division) was created, with the aim to create a tank unit that had strategic mobility. Furthermore, it was planned that the units would be capable of performing a surprise counterattack in the event of an enemy breakthrough, and they were equipped accordingly. The largest element was a *Schützen-Regiment* (SchtzRgt – rifle regiment) with two battalions (a PzDiv had two SchtzRgt) and a total of four *Schützen-Abteilungen* (SchtzAbt – rifle battalions). The reconnaissance elements were roughly comparable, and both had an artillery regiment.

Whereas the PzDiv had a PzBrig, the le Div had a PzAbt formed from four *leichte Panzerkompanien* (le PzKp – light tank companies) equipped exclusively with light tanks.

By 1938, four le Div had been formed, all of which were equipped with PzKpfw I and PzKpfw II and deployed in mass formations. But for an unknown reason, 3.le Div was issued with 55 PzKpfw 35(t).

A unique feature of the light divisions was that each battalion had a *Panzer-Transport-Kompanie* (tank transport company) equipped with FAUN (Fahrzeugfabriken Ansbach und Nürnburg GmbH) L 900-D567 heavy trucks and the 10,000kg-capacity *Sonderanhänger* (SdAnh – special purpose trailer) 115. This combination gave a light division the mobility, particularly on hard-surfaced roads, to be speedily re-deployed over long distances. Typically, a heavy truck would be loaded with a light tank and tow an SdAnh 115 carrying another. The four PzAbt in each le Div were identified by the suffix verl (*verlastet* – loaded).

In 1939, three – 2.le Div, 3.le Div and 4.le Div – of the four light divisions were combat ready. All were intended to be issued with PzKpfw I and PzKpfw II Ausf D *Schnellkampfwagen* (fast tanks) – both had a top speed of 55kph, making them the perfect vehicles for these highly mobile units. However, for an unknown reason, the actual allocation of types comprehensively differed to the KStN tables, with one of the units, 3.le Div, being issued with 23 PzKpfw II Ausf D and 55 PzKpfw 38(t).

Although it had been established as a light division in 1938, 1.le Div did not fit into this scheme. Even before the outbreak of hostilities, the unit was strengthened by the addition of another PzRgt, which meant it had three PzAbt and corresponded more to a standard armoured division. Also, a large number of PzKpfw 35(t) commandeered after the annexation of Czechoslovakia were used. The tank transport company was disbanded.

For various reasons, the decision to disband the le Div was taken before the outbreak of World War II. One reason could have been the economic situation in Germany, which had a detrimental effect on industry. Another was the requirement to supply the newly formed *Panzerwaffe* with better armed and armoured tanks with which to fight French and British armour in future battles. Finally, it was discovered during *Fall Weiss* (Plan White) that the poor condition of the roads in Poland – the majority were unpaved tracks – made it almost impossible to utilize the speed of the light tank formations. These same conditions identified many mechanical defects that resulted in far too many breakdowns. One positive point was that the 2cm KwK 30 L/55 auto cannon, mounted in the PzKpfw II, was very effective against hard targets and Polish armour.

By the start of *Fall Gelb* (Plan Yellow), the invasion of the Low Countries and France on 10 May 1940, all light divisions were to be reorganized as standard PzDiv. The reason for this decision remains unclear to this day.

Air Transport

It is worth remembering that in 1941, Germany became the first country in the world to have a strategic air transport capacity when the Messerschmitt Me 321 heavy transport glider entered service. The aircraft was produced to provide airlift capacity for *Unternehmen Seelöwe* (Operation Sealion), the invasion of Great Britain planned for September 1940. A total of 24 were built and entered service with four *Luftwaffe Transportgeschwader* (TrGeschw – transport squadrons), and were used for ferrying supplies to units fighting on the *Ost* (East) Front. Operational use was, however, hampered by the lack of a sufficiently powerful tug (towing) aircraft. As a result, Messerschmitt re-designed the airframe and fitted six French-manufactured Gnome et Rhône 14N air-cooled radial engines. The new heavy transport aircraft Me 323 D-1, known as *Gigant* (giant), entered service in September 1942 and had a range of some 800km. The type was first used to fly supplies and troop reinforcements to the *Panzerarmee Afrika* (Tank Army Africa) in Tunisia and, although slow – its cruising speed was 218kph – and vulnerable to attack by patrolling Allied fighter aircraft, its cargo flights over the Mediterranean continued. Urgently required tanks, armoured vehicles or artillery pieces (including those for the le Div) up to the weight of a PzKpfw IV flew almost directly to the battlefront. Production of the Me 323 ended in April 1943 after 198 had been built.

The Messerschmitt Me 323 *Gigant* transport aircraft, was operated by the *Luftwaffe* from airfields on Sicily to fly supplies to Axis forces in North Africa. The route across the eastern Mediterranean was constantly patrolled by Allied fighters based on Malta, and a significant number of this lumbering machine were shot down.

A PzKpfw II Ausf F of Panzer Lehr Regiment in the cargo bay of an Me 323. The tank weighed some 10,000kg and has been secured to the airframe by a number of wire strops. The huge aircraft could carry a payload of up to 22,000kg.

Condor Legion 3

On 17 July 1936, after several years of political unrest, the Spanish army, loyal to Nationalist *Generalissimo* Franco, rebelled against the ruling Republican left-wing government, igniting a brutal Civil War that would continue for three years.

Adolf Hitler, who had come to power in 1933, supported the Nationalists, but was reluctant to commit any military forces. Instead, he encouraged Benito Mussolini to send in Italian troops supported by some 150 Ansaldo-built *Carro Veloce* (CV – fast chariot) 33 light tanks – a type developed from the Carden-Loyd Tankette Mk VI.

However, Hitler soon reversed his decision and committed a number of transport, bomber, dive-bomber and fighter aircraft to aid Franco. He also dispatched a light tank detachment, issued with PzKpfw I Ausf A and an unknown number of PzKpfw I Ausf B – the first battlefield deployment of German tanks before World War II.

The Soviet Union, under Josef Stalin, supported the Republican side and subsequently delivered some 250 T-26 and 50 BT-5 tanks – both types were better armed than a PzKpfw I. The Soviets also supplied a significant number of infantry rifles and associated ammunition.

The fighting ceased on 26 January 1939 and, just a few days later, on 30 January 1939, the OKII issued a detailed appraisal of the performance of German forces and armaments in the conflict:

The Wehrmacht in the Spanish Civil War:

The main focus on the German participation lies with the *Luftwaffe*. The Panzer and anti-tank group advised and monitored those Spanish armoured forces issued with German and captured Soviet equipment. Here, to prevent improper use by the Spaniards, the store for tanks spare parts and anti-tank guns was controlled by our troops.

Opposite: Condor Legion PzKpfw I Ausf A tanks on a victory parade through the city of Valencia. At this point, the morale value of the light tanks was greater than their combat value. (Getty)

German army units were not deployed in Spain for combat but were used, to a limited extent, for reconnaissance.

Spanish units:

The organization of Spanish armed forces was very haphazard up until the end of 1936. Only after the failure at Madrid did the commanders of the Nationalist Army

Italian dictator Mussolini also supported the Spanish nationalists. These CV-33 tanks of the Italian *Corpo di Truppe Volontarie* (CVT - corps of volunteer troops) advance toward Republican positions near the city of Valencia. (Getty)

begin to establish new divisions. Here it must be emphasized that these 'divisions' do not correspond in any way to ours, which are organized according to modern battlefield practice.

Pointedly, at the beginning of the war, both parties lacked coordination between their infantry, artillery and armour arms. Tank attacks usually ended in failure, because infantry and artillery had not been trained to support the armour.

The Renault FT entered service with the French army in the latter stage of World War I and was exported to many nations. Although the light tank was obsolete by mid-1930, it was used by the Republican forces. (Getty)

Armoured forces:

Those outdated Spanish- and foreign-built armoured cars deployed on the battlefront have not proven to be effective, even for reconnaissance, due to their lack of off-road mobility. The Italian light machine gun tanks were used with much success, particularly for close reconnaissance when supporting infantry.

Only a small number, some 50 tanks, were used for offensive operations, usually without adequate support from artillery and well-trained infantry. Only a few points are worth mentioning in the tactics in the field due to the special conditions of this war.

Neither the leaders of Republican nor Nationalist forces succeeded in establishing a definitive plan for cooperation between their respective infantry, artillery and armoured units. On many occasions, a retreating Republican tank fell victim to petrol bombs and hand grenades thrown at close range by Nationalist troops.

The use of our machine gun tanks in battalion strength did not materialize but instead they were placed, in very small groups, under the direct command of an infantry unit, and used for armoured heavy support for troops advancing from one target to another. The PzKpfw I could not be deployed to lead an attack since it was vulnerable to shell and armour-piercing infantry ammunition. Although first acknowledged in World War I, it was confirmed in the inter-war period that, in a tank-versus-tank shoot out, a gun-armed type was considerably superior than that armed with a machine gun – this proved to be correct in Spain. Conversely, it was shown that our 7.92mm armour-piercing ammunition fired from a machine gun easily penetrated a Soviet-built tank (13mm armour) at a range of 100m. This fact and the destructive effect of our 3.7cm PaK meant that a Republican tank usually came to halt at a range of some 1,000m before opening fire. Because they were used in this way, these artillery shells were repeatedly referred to as the decisive weapon of the Reds.

The tank is very effective when deployed for a surprise mass attack against already shattered enemy front-line positions. Armour protection and weaponry are more important than speed and range (*). Many tank attacks made without the support of gun-armed types and supporting infantry failed miserably.

The Soviet Union sent a considerable number of T-26 M 1933 to Spain in support of the Republican forces. Although classified as a light tank, it mounted a very powerful and effective 45mm gun. When positioned out of range to enemy artillery, it could be a vital weapon on the battlefront.

As the Civil War progressed, many T-26 were captured and used by the Nationalist forces. The powerfully armed type was often deployed to lead an attack, leaving the PzKpfw I Ausf A to deal with dug-in infantry. The platoon is led by a kl PzBefWg; note the commander is using a *Sprechschlauch* (speaking tube) to converse with his driver. (Getty)

The hot and dry Spanish climate severely affected the mechanically vulnerable armoured vehicles. This PzKpfw I broke down due to a gearbox problem, so the yellow/red breakdown flag was raised in accord with German regulations.

Accurate fire was almost impossible from a light tank when in motion. At the same time, they could be defeated by machine guns firing armour-piercing ammunition. In reality, the light tank is only effective as a flamethrower carrier. Overall, when deployed in small numbers and without artillery and infantry support, the light tank has proven to be inneffective.

Vehicles:

The Krupp- and Maybach-powered PzKpfw I (**) proved, in the opinion of the troops, to be mechanically reliable. The Ausf A achieved 5,000km–8,000km, the Ausf B from 2,000km–5,000km before overhaul (***).

The SdKfz 7 [Kraus-Maffei] has proven to be ideal as a towing vehicle for our *Flugzeugabwehrkanone* [FlaK – anti-aircraft gun] unit after their Maybach engines

A kl PzBefWg and a PzKpfw I Ausf A in a Spanish town as the fighting ended. Both vehicles have Nationalist identification markings painted on the superstructure. The German tank force sent to Spain was code-named *Gruppe Drohne* (group drone).

had been adjusted to run on higher-octane fuel.

A *kleiner Flammenwerfer* [small flamethrower] can easily be installed in the PzKpfw I by replacing the right-hand side machine gun. But in view of the high losses experienced, the weapon must have a longer range.

Recovery:

The *Transportkolonne* [transport column] was made up of one passenger car, two *Motorrad mit Beiwagen* [motorcycle with sidecar (combination)] 14 VOMAG and ten Büssing-NAG diesel-powered trucks, 19 *Tiefladeanhänger* [low-loader trailer] 115 and four *Laderampen* [loading ramps].

Note: On many occasions, the damaged tank could not be recovered because the trailer lacked sufficient ground clearance, especially over rock-strewn or uneven terrain. Allocating a few more SdKfz 7 tractors would be the simplest way of alleviating this problem. In another incident, where a PzKpfw I had left the road and slid 150m down an embankment, the recovery was extremely difficult and took a few days, since none of our heavy trucks were fitted with a winch.

(*) This regularly propounded assumption was, and still is, most certainly based on experience gained during World War I. But if this was embraced without restraint, every increase in armour (combat weight) would result in an enemy deploying an even more powerful anti-tank weapon. Ultimately, the armour-versus-anti-tank weapon race cannot be won by the tank.

(**) PzKpfw I Ausf A and PzKpfw I Ausf B.

(***) This statement seems optimistic and cannot be confirmed.

Among the tanks sent by the German *Reich* to strengthen Nationalist forces were an unknown number of PzKpfw I Ausf B. The type was powered by a 3,970cc Maybach NL38 TR six-cylinder water-cooled engine which, being longer than the Krupp 305, required the hull to be lengthened and a fifth running wheel fitted.

The evaluation of the experiences made during the Spanish Civil War was of great importance to German military planners, since the conflict served as a testing ground for both the *Luftwaffe* and the *Wehrmacht*. The tactical principles for armoured formations, propounded by Heinz Guderian in the early 1930s, had been tried on the Spanish battleground and found, in the main, to have worked.

The fact that the Soviet-supplied gun-armed light tank was superior to the MG-armed PzKpfw I is not surprising; even German military planners were aware of this before the war. Nevertheless, the report points to some offensive use of the PzKpfw I (omitted by Nationalist forces). Ideally, any attack involving armoured vehicles should begin with a preparatory barrage, by the divisional artillery, to effectively destroy any anti-tank weapons. Any engagement at close range must always be supported by infantry to protect the tanks from enemy close-combat squads.

The report emphasizes the performance of the Italian-built CV-33 for close-in reconnaissance, but does not state whether the PzKpfw I was used for the same purpose.

The Soviet-supplied T-26 and BT-5 tanks had relatively high mobility and mounted a 45mm gun designed to fire destructive high-explosive ammunition – the anti-tank round easily knocked out any of the armoured vehicles deployed by Nationalist forces. Conversely, the armour (13mm maximum) on the Soviet-built tanks was decidedly inadequate and frequently penetrated by armour-piercing infantry ammunition.

In reality, Republican forces were perceived as inferior, being commanded by inexperienced officers and having artillery, mechanized and infantry units manned by poorly trained soldiers. Despite each unit being supplied with modern equipment, much was lost on the battlefront due to tactical errors made by inexperienced commanders.

Škoda and ČKD 4

In 1938, Czechoslovakia, which came into being after the collapse of the Habsburg monarchy (1282–1918), had an efficient industry with a number of companies producing passenger cars for the mass market, as well as two large armaments companies: Škoda in Plzeň (Pilsen) and Praga, a subsidiary of Českomoravská Kolben-Daněk (ČKD), in Praha (Prague). Both companies had begun the design and development of tanks in the early 1930s.

First Light Tanks

In 1929, a delegation from the Czechoslovak army, led by Lieutenant Colonel Bedrich Albrecht, visited the British engineering conglomerate Vickers-Armstrongs Limited to inspect the Carden-Loyd Mk VI Tankette. The officer and his team were impressed with the type, which seemed like an ideal support vehicle for advancing infantry. Also, they appreciated that the tankette was simple to construct, meaning it was relatively inexpensive.

In 1930, ČKD procured three vehicles and subsequently negotiated a licence from Vickers-Armstrongs to manufacture and develop the type. By the end of 1930, Praga had produced four prototype vehicles, designated CL-P (Carden-Loyd-Praga), for evaluation trials. Even before these had concluded, the Czechoslovak military expressed serious concerns – a number of which were mechanical – with the operation of the type.

The engine, positioned in the centre of the fighting compartment, produced a lot of noise, excess heat and exhaust fumes to the detriment of the two-man crew – a common problem with a tankette. Crew comfort was also badly affected by the running gear's lack of effective suspension.

When the type was being driven on unsurfaced roads, country lanes or rough tracks, a number of serious weaknesses became obvious. Any deep ruts encountered seriously affected the steering and often led to a track being

Opposite: A column of LT vz 35 light tanks on a training ground before annexation. The vehicles are painted in the standard tri-colour camouflage scheme adopted by the Czechoslovak army.

Above: In the early 1930s, Škoda developed the MUV-4 tankette; the resemblance to a Carden-Loyd product is obvious. (Czech MoD)

Right: After initially gaining experience producing tankettes, ČKD developed the LT vz 34, a light tank that was fitted with a rotatable turret and mounted an effective 37mm Škoda ÚV vz. 34 cannon.

thrown, immobilizing the vehicle. The same often occurred when the tankette was being driven across sloping terrain. Finally, the CL-P had poor ground clearance, so it was even possible for a medium-sized rock to damage the engine and transmission housing.

Since no production order was forthcoming from the Czechoslovak military after the trials, ČKD decided to undertake an almost complete redesign of the vehicle to eliminate the faults found with the prototypes. The superstructure, fabricated from riveted armour plates, was significantly enlarged by moving the engine to a separate compartment in the rear – the two-man crew would no longer be affected by engine-generated heat and fumes. The increased interior space not only improved crew comfort, but also provided stowage space for extra machine gun ammunition. Finally, the running gear was redesigned to be more reliable and fitted with improved suspension.

As a result, the Czechoslovak *Ministerstvo Národni Obrany* (MNO – ministry of national defence) ordered 70 vehicles under the designation P-I or *Lehký Tank vzor* (LT vz – light tank model) 33. All attempts to market these vehicles internationally failed.

Originally, it had been proposed for Škoda to produce a copy of the Carden-Loyd Tankette, but in 1934 the company independently developed a machine gun carrier, the *Malý Utočný Vůz* (MUV – small assault vehicle) 4. In 1935, the company utilized the chassis to design and produce the *Škodová* (S – Škoda car) 1, a small tank armed with a 37mm cannon, but only a small number were completed, including eight supplied to Yugoslavia.

After producing versions of the Carden-Loyd Tankette under licence, ČKD designed and built the AH-IV light tank, which was fitted with Christie-type torsion bar running gear.

In 1934, Škoda developed the SU light tank. A year later, they began producing the first of the 202 LT vz 35 ordered by the Czechoslovak army. In 1936, the company produced 136, designated R-2, for Romania.

Škoda LT vz 35

In 1933, the MNO issued their specification for a heavier, well-armed and highly manoeuvrable tank. Although ČKD initially showed an interest, the company was informed that Škoda had been given the contract for design and development of the vehicle.

Just one year later, Škoda delivered a prototype of their *Stredni Útočný* (SU – medium assault vehicle) that not only met the specification, but was also relatively inexpensive to manufacture. The layout of the vehicle basically corresponded to that of the Vickers 6-ton Type B tank then in service with the British Army.

The hull and superstructure were fabricated from armour plates riveted together and the vehicle mounted a 37mm Škoda A3 gun in a turret positioned in the centre of the superstructure. A 7.9mm Zbrojvka Brno (ZB) vz 38 machine gun, for self-defence, was installed in the hull, adjacent to the driver.

The running gear was similar to that on the Vickers tank: two leaf-sprung bogies carrying eight small running wheels on each side that distributed the weight of the vehicle evenly. In contrast to the Vickers tank, however, the engine, transmission and final drives were positioned in the rear of the hull – a forward-thinking space-saving solution.

Škoda also developed self-propelled guns based on the SU, but these were not of interest to the MNO.

As the development trials continued, an improved prototype, designated the LT vz 35, was delivered at the end of 1934. The type was extensively tested until 1936, during which time a number of defects were identified, especially with the unconventional pneumatically powered steering.

Although the many of the mechanical defects could not be resolved by December 1936, the MNO decided to order a further number of prototype vehicles. However, political relations with Nazi Germany continued to seriously deteriorate, causing the MNO to insist that ČKD must be included in the programme. Unfortunately, the company's initial cooperation with Škoda did not run smoothly.

In 1937, both companies began, with some urgency, to mass produce the LT vz. 35 despite problems with the running gear remaining unresolved. This resulted in the MNO declaring the vehicle not combat ready. A number of modifications were applied throughout 1938 and, although some problems were rectified, many of the tanks involved in the reliability trials achieved more than 2,000km of running without major repairs.

The LT vz 35 was, in many respects, an advanced design. A four-cylinder Škoda T/110 engine, along with the transmission and final drives, was housed in a bay in the rear of the hull. Importantly, this allowed the designers to increase the size of the fighting compartment. Another advance feature was the use of compressed air to operate the clutch, gear change and steering brakes; this not only saved space, but also reduced driver fatigue.

ČKD sold 48 AH-IV to Sweden, where they were designated Strv m/37 and fitted with a Volvo FC ČKD six-cylinder petrol engine and a number of modifications, including a larger turret mounting two machine guns. (Swedish Army Museum)

The LT vz 35 was fitted with pin-type tracks which had a service life of more than 6,000km. The final drive sprockets and idler wheels were fitted with guide flanges to prevent the tracks from being thrown off and immobilizing the tank.

The hull and superstructure of the LT vz 35 were assembled from armour plates riveted to internal steel frames. However, this type of fabrication had some dangerous disadvantages.

If a rivet was hit, it could become loose and fly around the fighting compartment, damaging equipment and causing injuries that were often fatal to those inside. Also, the joints between the plates presented a weak point and torsional stiffness was less than that provided by a welded construction. However, despite arc welding being used by heavy industry, riveted construction was a tried and tested method that many manufacturers considered to be more economical. By 1935, arc welding had become the accepted method for fabricating armoured bodywork.

Production of the LT vz 35 ended after some 300 of the type had been completed. In 1937, all were issued by the Czechoslovak army to equip three tank regiments.

In 1942, Germany Reich delivered 35 PzKpfw 35(t) to Romania, but by that time the type was hopelessly outdated.

ČKD LT vz 38

In 1934, ČKD independently began the design and development of a completely new light tank, the AH-IV. At the time, it was unique for having very simple, but robust, running gear – each pair of the eight road wheels was fitted with a leaf spring. This arrangement not only allowed the tank to be driven at high speed (even cross-country), but it was also extremely reliable and easy to maintain. The company delivered 50 of the type to Persia (Iran), 35 to Romania and 48 to Sweden. The latter two countries continued to build the AH-IV under licence as the R-1 and Strv m/37, respectively. (Ethiopia ordered 20 of the type on 24 June 1948.)

In 1937, the MNO issued the specification for a new type of light tank and requested, with some urgency, companies to tender for the design, development and the production of 400 vehicles. This sudden decision was most probably influenced by rising tensions along the border with Nazi Germany.

As a result, ČKD utilized its experience with the AH-IV and quickly produced the *Těžký Nakladni* (TN – truck engine) and *Housenka* (H – caterpillar) tracks, subsequently known as the TN-H. The type restored ČKD to its position as the leading tank design and production company in Czechoslovakia.

The AH-IV was further developed and exported to several foreign nations, including Switzerland. Their military ordered 26 LTH, but all were to be delivered dismantled and without engines. On delivery, all were fitted with a Saurer diesel engine. The LTH entered Swiss army service as the *Panzer* 39.

After the occupation of Czechoslovakia, all existing LT vz 35 were commandeered by the German forces. After a number of modifications, the type entered service as PzKpfw 35(t). Here, two of this type and five PzBefWg 35(t) are parked in the yard at the barracks of PzRgt 11.

Right: In 1938, following a request from the Czechoslovak MNO, ČKD began the development of the TNH (LT vz 38) light tank. Basically, it was an improved LTH fitted with torsion bar running gear. The TNH was armed with a 37mm Škoda 37mm ÚV vz. 38 main gun mounted in a rotatable turret.

Left: In 1942, ČKD, although under German control, granted a licence for the TNH tank to be built by Scania-Vabis AB at their factory in Södertälje, Sweden. Designated Strv m/41 by the Swedish army, it was armed with a 37mm Bofors m/36 cannon and two 8mm m/38 MG. A total of 238 were ordered and many remained in service during the 1950s.

Mechanically, the TN-H was very similar to an AH-IV, except for the running gear which now had four large-diameter road wheels on each side. The hull and superstructure were specifically designed to be much larger, but were again fabricated by using rivets.

Unlike the LT vz 35, the engine – a Praga TN/II – was fitted in the rear of the hull and connected to the transmission and final drives at the front by a Cardan-type shaft that passed under the fighting compartment.

The vehicle carried a crew of three and was armed with a Škoda 3.7cm A7 gun and a 7.9mm ZB vz 53 machine gun mounted in the turret. An identical machine gun was also installed in the front plate next to the driver.

After being accepted for service by the MNO, all production TN-H were designated as the LT vz 38.

In the meantime, the political situation continued to deteriorate. Czech-Sudetenland was home to a significant German-speaking minority and was a region of great economic and cultural importance. Hitler adeptly used nationalist ideology to create unrest and further his expansionist policies.

The process began with a targeted propaganda campaign by the NSDAP to support the Sudeten Germans. At the end of June 1938, German forces held manoeuvres near the border; a clear provocation. On 28 September, a four-power conference was convened to prevent Hitler from escalating the situation. On 30 September, the Munich Agreement was signed by Great Britain, France, Italy and Germany (tragically excluding Czechoslovakia), ceding the whole of Sudetenland to the *Reich*. As a result, German forces crossed into the region on 1 October 1938. However, Hitler had a very different itinerary.

Far left: After it had been modified to carry a crew of four, production of the TNH began in 1939 at Czechoslovak factories controlled by German authorities. The type was subsequently designated PzKpfw 38(t) and, as with the LT vz 35, fitted with a German-made radio.

As a result of Munich, President Beneš was forced into exile and travelled to London. The weakened government could not prevent Slovak entities in the east of the country from preparing and finally carrying out a secession.

Hitler now made preparations to invade and occupy the *Rest-Tschechei* (rest of Czechoslovakia), and on 15 March 1939, a triumphant Führer led his forces into the city of Prague. Soon after the occupation, officers from the *Wehrmacht* began to assemble an inventory of Czechoslovak army equipment suitable for German service. At the same time, manufacturers, including Škoda, came under the control of Reichswerke Hermann Göring.

Among those types examined, the LT vz 35 attracted the most attention, since it was not known to the Germans.

Dipl Ing. T. Icken, regimental engineer of the PzRgt 6, wrote the following note:

On 15 March 1939, the 3.PzDiv, to which the PzRgt 6 belonged, marched into the 'golden city' of Prague. At the end of March 1939, as a regimental engineer of PzRgt 6, I was commissioned to inspect the Czechoslovak-built LT vz 35 light tanks at the Milowitz military training area. Together with other tank officers, I carried out test drives with several vehicles on the obstacle course at the vehicle testing station. Czechoslovak officers obligingly gave answers about the main battle tanks unknown to us.

I described the LT vz 35 as a usable and mobile vehicle with considerable firepower (one 3.7cm gun and two machine guns) and a mechanically interesting gear change and steering gear. The riveted armour plates were disadvantageous because they were more vulnerable when hit. The 3.PzDiv was informed accordingly.

The Czechoslovak officers at Milowitz reported that the company ČKD in Prague was about to start series production of a newly developed armoured fighting vehicle that has a combat weight of 9,700kg and the same armament as the Lt vz 35. The *Wehrmacht* was not aware of this detail.

After our trip to Milowitz, which we took armed only with hand weapons and in a *Kübelwagen* [bucket-seat car], we then visited the manufacturing facilities of Praga [the company had merged with ČKD in 1929]. It was well known that it had been manufacturing motor vehicles since 1907 and had, up until 1918, supplied passenger cars, trucks and artillery tractors to the Austro-Hungarian army.

The factory buildings appeared solid despite having been built at around the turn of the century. We later noticed that although the machinery was also outdated, quality work was still being done. The factory watchman informed us, in broken German, that there was no work at the moment due to the factory being temporarily closed. But, as a result of our insistence, he agreed to telephone some engineers who worked in the design and production offices. Immediately after they arrived, we began a tour of the factory, which included inspecting numerous machine shops, where various parts were produced, followed by the fabrication and assembly hall. Although they had not been given official permission, the engineers freely discussed with us the newly developed tank.

The LT vz 38 was well-designed and fitted with simple leaf-spring suspension and four large road wheels. It also had a newly developed Wilson-type preselector gearbox and advanced air-assisted steering gear/brakes, as well as a powerful 3.7cm gun.

Early delivery would be achievable, since a working production line had already been established; in fact, there were a number of tanks at various stages of assembly.

After the visit, I delivered my detailed assessment of the newly developed LT vz 38 to Major Thomale (*), the tank officer at the OKH.

(*)Thomale headed a team of officers assembled from In.6, the HWa and other procurement authorities sent to Prague after the occupation.

In April 1939, the HWa issued a production order to ČKD for some 100 of the type, which the company subsequently completed without any problems and delivered on time in August 1939. All LT vz 38 delivered to the *Wehrmacht* were designated PzKpfw 38(t) – the (t) indicates *tschechisch*: Czechoslovak origin.

In reality, however, the HWa never really supported the PzKpfw 38(t) since the department neither wrote the specification nor initiated the design, and was not involved in the development process.

During the Polish campaign, the German army had some 57 PzKpfw 38(t) tanks, which were used in the 3.le Div. Initially, a Czechoslovak-made combat antenna was installed on the left side of the superstructure.

German Service

The exact sequence of decisions made after the annexation of Czechoslovakia with regard to commandeered Czechoslovak army equipment cannot be fully described or evaluated due to a lack of contemporary documents. However, it is interesting to note that the Czechoslovak military had already recognized the value of effective communications on the battlefront and had radio equipment installed.

The first change that was ordered in line with German operational requirements involved manning, since both the LT vz 35 and LT vz 38 were originally designed to have a crew of three: a driver, a radio operator and a commander, who also had to aim, load and fire the turret-mounted weapons while guiding the vehicle. This totally contradicted current German practice: the PzKpfw III Ausf A, which had comparable firepower, was manned by a crew

The roadway has collapsed under the combined weight of a Bussing-NAG *Typ* 900 heavy truck loaded with a PzKpfw 38(t). Men from the transport company attached to PzAbt 67 (3.le PzDiv), begin the difficult task of off-loading the tank. The incident has attracted a number of onlookers, including a *Kradmelder* (dispatch rider) wearing his distinctive long, leather coat.

of five – *Panzerführer* (commander), *Fahrer* (driver), *Funker* (radio operator), *Richtschütze* (gunner) and *Ladeschütze* (loader). The gunner and loader operated the main gun and turret machine gun, while the hull MG was fired by the radio operator, leaving the commander to concentrate on the battlefield.

Consequently, the superstructure on both the LT vz 35 and the LT vz 38 was redesigned to make space in the fighting compartment for a loader/gunner.

The original Czechoslovak-manufactured radio was replaced by German radio equipment. Initially, all tanks were fitted with a Fu 2 receiver, whereas those for a *Kompaniefuhrer* (company commander) were fitted with a Fu 5 transceiver. After a short period, all tanks would be equipped with the Fu 5, while the command vehicles received an additional Fu 2. Eventually, as the supply situation improved, all tanks would be equipped with a Fu 5 and Fu 2 as standard.

Both the PzKpfw 35(t) and Pzkpfw 38(t) were also produced as a PzBefWg with more powerful radio equipment. Vehicles at battalion staff or regimental staff level were designated SdKfz 267 and fitted with the Fu 5 and a long-range Fu 8. Those SdKfz 268 that were issued to *Fliegerverbindungs-Offiziere* (FliVO – ground-to-air liaison officers) were equipped with a Fu 7 and a Fu 5.

Both types carried a 2m *Stabantenne* (rod antenna) and a very conspicuous *Rahmenantenne* (frame-type aerial), which was mounted on the engine compartment cover plate when a Fu 8 was fitted. The turret on both versions was non-rotatable, and a dummy gun barrel was fitted to represent the main armament.

The modification and PzBefWg programme were carried out in a relatively short time, and this was probably due to a plentiful supply of new tanks available to the OrgAbt. Other factors could have been that the date for the invasion of Poland (1 September 1939) had already been set and that, in March 1939, only 60 of the 3.7cm-armed PzKpfw III Ausf A had been delivered and production of the type remained slow.

A document produced by the HWa, dated 15 January 1936, details the planned tank force (including reserves) for 1 October, 1939:

	Target October 1939	Actual September 1939
MG and 2cm PzKpfw	1,369	1,668
3.7cm PzKpfw III	3,139	98
7.5cm PzKpfw IV	780	211

The discrepancy is obvious and is indicative of the inability of German armament manufacturers to even come close to achieving the required production figures.

In this context, the availability of a large number of mechanically reliable Czechoslovak-built tanks would most certainly be welcomed by those responsible in the OrgAbt.

All available LT vz 35 – now designated was PzKpfw 35(t) - were delivered to *Wehrmacht* workshops in Germany for modifications, including those for conversion to SdKfz 267 or SdKfz 268 standard.

By 1 September 1939, a total of 202 PzKpfw 35(t) were available to the *Panzerwaffe* and 164 had already been issued to front-line units.

Since both the PzKpfw 35(t) and the PzKpfw 38(t) mounted a 3.7cm gun, German military planners were confident that both types could be used as a substitute for the PzKpfw III in a PzDiv. This made it possible to assemble an

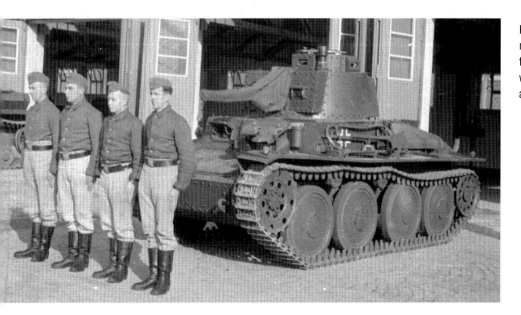

Roll call at PzAbt 67. A new PzKpfw 38(t) with its four-man crew. The main weapon is covered with a tarpaulin.

entire armoured unit equipped with Czechoslovak-built tanks. The 1.le Div was formed with PzAbt 65 issued with 37 PzKpfw 35(t) and two PzBefwg 35(t), and PzRgt 11 issued with 75 PzKpfw 35(t) and six PzBefWg 35(t). The division was also issued with PzKpfw I, PzKpfw II and PzKpfw IV.

In early 1940, 1.le Div was reformed as 6.PzDiv and began training for *Fall Gelb* (Plan Yellow), the invasion of the Low Countries and, ultimately, France.

For *Unternehmen Barbarossa*, 6.PzDiv was attached to *Heeresgruppe* (HG – army group) *Nord* (north) and then HG *Mitte* (centre) for the Battle of Moscow, where it was virtually annihilated. The remnants were then sent to France for rest and replenishment. It was here that the few remaining PzKpfw 35(t) would be withdrawn from front-line service. Eventually, the division would be issued with new equipment, PzKpfw III Ausf J to Ausf L (5cm KwK 39 L/60) and PzKpfw IV Ausf F (7.5cm KwK L/43).

LT vz 35 (Czechoslovak Service)

Year:	1938
Weight:	9,700kg
Crew:	Three
Armament:	One 37mm Škoda A; two 7.9mm ZB vz 37
Armour:	16mm–25mm
Engine:	120hp Škoda TII/0, four-cylinder water-cooled petrol
Range (maximum):	190km
Speed (maximum):	34kph

PzKpfw 38(t)

Although production of the LT vz 35 had ended in 1937, the *Wehrmacht* continued to utilize the type for any suitable task. But for the LT vz 38, the OrgAbt had more far-reaching plans and saw the type as having a much higher combat potential.

The company ČKD, which in the meantime had come under German control and been renamed Böhmisch-Mährische Motorenfabrik (BMM), was ordered to commence production. A first series of 150 vehicles was manufactured between May and November 1939.

During the attack on Poland, only 3.le Div could be equipped and was issued with 55 PzKpfw 38(t) and two PzBefWg 38(t).

As production continued, front-line crews complained about the lack of effective armour protection, but found the type to be reliable and have adequate performance. By May 1940, a total of 260 PzKpfw 38(t) had been delivered.

During *Fall Gelb*, both 7.PzDiv and 8.PzDiv were issued with the PzKpfw 38(t) (some 100 each and a number of PzBefWg), but 6.PzDiv was still equipped with PzKpfw 35(t).

During the June 1941 attack on the Soviet Union, four armoured divisions were equipped with PzKpfw 38(t): 7.PzDiv, 8.PzDiv, 19.PzDiv and 20.PzDiv had some 400 in total: 6.PzDiv was still in action with 155 PzKpfw 35(t).

The importance of these Czechoslovak-built tanks commandeered by the *Wehrmacht* cannot be overestimated, since both types filled the role of medium battle tanks in a number of Panzer divisions. In 1941, during the initial phase of *Unternehmen Barbarossa*, crews continued to complain about weak armour and ballistically poor armament that was virtually ineffective against the armour of a Red Army T-34. Despite these problems, the PzKpfw 38(t) continued to be used by front-line units during the summer attack on the Caucasus in 1942. This was due to German industry being unable to produce sufficient numbers of the latest versions of the PzKpfw III and PzKpfw IV, respectively armed with the 5cm KwK 39 L/60 and 7.5cm KwK L/48 long-barrelled guns – at that time, both were the most effective tanks in *Wehrmacht* service.

All production of the PzKpfw 38(t) ended in June 1942, after more than 1,400 had been delivered to the *Panzerwaffe*, but officials in the HWa had already noted that the reliable and robust chassis would be ideal for the production of self-propelled guns, including the *Jagdpanzer* 38 *Hetzer*.

Opposite: Unlike most German tanks in service during the late 1930s, the PzKpfw 35(t) and PzKpfw 38(t) were assembled using heavy steel rivets. Note the lightning bolt symbol, painted on the side of the turret, indicating that the vehicle has been prepared for the installation of radio equipment.

LT vz 35 (Czechoslovak Service)

Year:	1937
Weight:	9,700kg
Crew:	Three
Armament:	One 37mm Škoda A7; two 7.9mm ZB vz 37
Armour:	16mm–25mm
Engine:	120hp Praga TN/II, six-cylinder water-cooled petrol
Range (maximum:	250km
Speed (maximum):	42kph

The PzTrspKp of
3.le Div was equipped
with Faun L 900 heavy
trucks and SdAnh 115
trailers. This made it
possible to transport
two PzKpfw 38(t) over
long distances without
any stress to the engine,
transmission or
running gear.

108677

Poland and Beyond **5**

Shortly before the beginning of World War II, the number of tank-versus-tank fighting types – the 3.7cm-armed PzKpfw III, PzKpfw 35(t) and PzKpfw 38(t) – could not be increased significantly. Some 300 of all three types were available, and this number also only came about after the invasion of Czechoslovakia. Production of the PzKpfw III had begun at a slow rate with just 87 being delivered by September 1939.

The majority of the PzDiv involved in the invasion only had light tank companies and since these could not be fully equipped with the required number of 3.7cm-armed tanks, they were issued with light tanks: 1,000 PzKpfw I and 1,150 PzKpfw II.

After the end of *Fall Weiße* (Plan White), extensive after-action reports were written by officers at all levels. Many dealt with how a unit was organized and the failure or success of battle tactics, whereas others evaluated the combat effectiveness of their troops and also the mechanical reliability of their equipment, including vehicles.

While a number of reports were delivered by the commanders of PzKpfw III and PzKpfw IV medium tanks units, this does not apply to those involving the PzKpfw I and PzKpfw II. It is quite possible that the commanders expected the light tanks to be phased out soon and therefore saw little reason to elucidate on their experiences.

From a report sent by PzRgt 6 (3.PzDiv) on 2 October 1939:

PzKpfw I is obsolete.
PzKpfw II urgently requires better vision devices for the *Panzerführer* [tank commander].
PzKpfw III and PzKpfw IV are effective, but both require stronger armour.
The kl PzBefWg requires a rotatable turret to make it truly effective on the battlefront.

Opposite: Many roads in rural Poland were little more than gravel-surfaced tracks, completely unsuitable for the transit of even a light tank. Here, the surface has collapsed under the weight of a PzKpfw 35(t). Recovery would be a lengthy process.

The PzKpfw I Ausf A was normally armed with two 7.92mm MG 13k (*kurzrohr* – short barrel). However, this tank has been fitted with two standard 7.92mm MG 13 that are identifiable by their significantly longer barrel, fitted with a large muzzle flash diffuser.

This assessment is not surprising: the PzKpfw I armed with two machine guns had little firepower and armour that only protected the crew from light infantry weapons. The lack of an all-round view for the commander of a PzKpfw II had been recognized for a long time and the HWa had already initiated appropriate measures. However, it would not be until October 1940 that an improved hatch with eight vision blocks became available and was progressively delivered to front-line units or field workshops.

It is interesting that, in his report, the commander of PzRgt 6 suggested the installation of a turret periscope manufactured by the Czechoslovak company Optikotechn in Přerov (Opticotechna GmbH, Prerau) on the PzKpfw II.

He also submitted his suggestions for improvement:

> The staffs of the armoured brigade and regiment should be equipped with their own tanks for close-in, combat reconnaissance. I suggest the PzKpfw II be fitted with fast-type tracks and a cupola or a Czechoslovak-manufactured periscope for the commander.

This reference undoubtedly refers to those PzKpfw II Ausf D in service with 3.le Div. However, the HWa already had other plans for the type.

The tactical and operational units in the *Aufklärung* (reconnaissance) departments of all German divisions were not issued with tanks, instead they had four-, six- or eight-wheeled *Panzerspähwagen* (armoured cars). These vehicles had been developed to operate on well-made road surfaces and had limited off-road mobility; a fact that became evident in Poland. In principle, a light tank such as the PzKpfw II would have been ideal for these purposes.

From February 1940, the organization of armoured divisions began to change as more tanks became available. The *leichte Panzerkompanien* (le PzKp – light tank companies) and *mittlere Panzerkompanien* (m PzKp – medium tank companies) could now be issued with increasing numbers of PzKpfw III (le PzKp) and PzKpfw IV (m PzKp), whereas the number of PzKpfw I was noticeably reduced. Any remaining PzKpfw II were used for a variety of tasks, including battlefield reconnaissance – a task for which a purpose-built type had not yet been developed.

The kl PzBefWg (SdKfz 265) command tank continued to be criticized, as in this note from PzRgt 8, dated October 1939:

20 April 1938: *Wehrmacht* tanks were often used for propaganda purposes, as here during a parade to mark the birthday of Adolf Hitler. The tank has the pre-war two-tone camouflage scheme of *dunkel braus* (dark brown) patches over standard *dunkel grau* (dark grey).

Right: During the invasion of Poland, the PzKpfw I was frequently deployed, with much success, against enemy reconnaissance patrols or supply columns. Polish forces simply did not have sufficient anti-tank units to protect every action.

Below: Elements of le PzKp type a, attached to 1.PzDiv, prepare for an attack. The column of PzKpfw I and PzKpfw II is led by a better-armed and -armoured PzKpfw IV.

Above: The deployment of the kl PzBefWg was not, at first, a success since it had poor firepower and armour. Also, the height of the superstructure made it easy to spot for enemy gunners.

Left: The idler wheels and five-spoke road wheels allowed mud to build up on the running gear. In freezing conditions, this often caused a track to fail. Here, a PzKpfw I Ausf A from PzAbt 23 is being thoroughly cleaned.

The kl PzBefWg is useless and should be replaced, with some urgency, by a suitably modified PzKpfw II; an Ausf C or Ausf D would be expedient.

In January 1940, after the invasion of Poland had concluded, PzRgt 31 (5.PzDiv) carried out a transfer march under winter conditions that also served as a trial to gain experience for similar operations in the future.

During the march, problems were identified on both the PzKpfw I and PzKpfw II. The intense cold resulted in the welded seams on the superstructure of a

The recovery services of the PzDiv had variety of flatbed trailers. The lighter SdAnh115 had a 10,000kg capacity that was sufficient to transport a PzKpfw I Ausf B. The trailer is attached to an SdKfz 6 medium half-track tractor.

PzKpfw II becoming brittle and fractured. Since an immediate repair was impossible, the tank would have to be loaded on a trailer and taken to the nearest workshop.

Another problem revealed by the conditions was that the tracks did not have sufficient grip on the ice and snow, causing many tanks to skid and slide into a roadside ditch. As an experiment, some track links were reversed and the guide teeth shortened to provide better grip. Although this alteration was somewhat effective, it drastically reduced the service life of the rubber tyres on the road wheels.

Right: A PzKpfw II Ausf c from PzAbt 65 (1.le Div) is loaded on to a heavy truck from the PzTrspKp.

Below: A *Panzer-Pionier-Bataillon* (PzPiBtl – armoured engineer battalion) was responsible for bridging obstacles. Here, a PzKpfw II Ausf c crosses a bridge fabricated from wood. The *Balkenkreuz* has a white outline and a yellow interior.

Left: As German forces advanced deeper into Poland, they were confronted by a vast number of water obstacles. Here, a PzKpfw II crosses a shallow stream as men from a PzPiBtl begin building a bridge.

Below: The open inspection hatch on this PzKpfw II Ausf suggests that the vehicle has crashed due to brake or transmission failure.

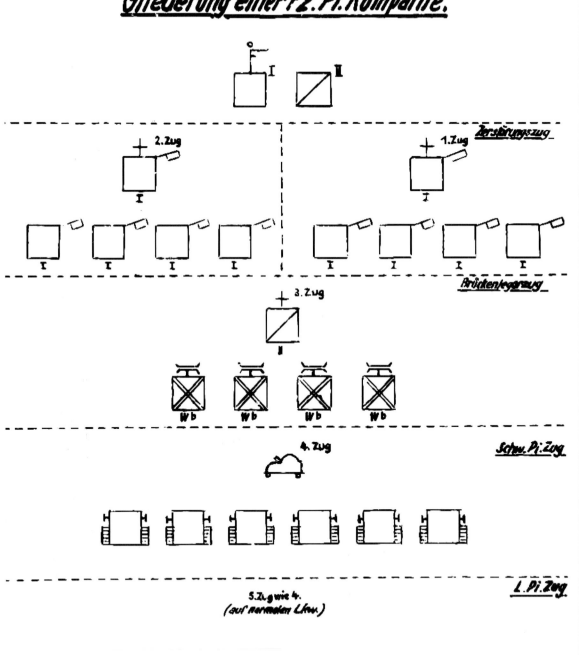

PzKpfw I – New Uses

From 1940, the PzKpfw I began to be increasingly used for new tasks within the tank units. In February 1940, instructions were issued to incorporate *Panzerpionier-Kompanien* (PzPiKp – armoured engineer companies) into the *Pionier-Bataillone* (PiBtl – engineer battalions) in a PzDiv. These vehicles were to be fitted with whatever special-purpose equipment required by the PzPi to fulfil their important tasks. The selection of a tracked armoured chassis not only provided protection for the crew, but also improved off-road mobility.

These PzPiKp were created by the 1.PzDiv, 2.PzDiv, 3.Pz\Div, 4.PzDiv and 10.PzDiv by reorganizing existing sub-units, whereas 5.PzDiv, 6.PzDiv, 7.PzDiv, 8.PzDiv and 9.PzDiv organized theirs by assembling new formations. The company staff was issued with a PzKpfw I and a PzKpfw II. The 1.*Zug* (Zg – platoon) and 2.Zg were designated as *Zerstörerzüge* (destroyer platoons), and each was issued with five PzKpfw I fitted with a rear-mounted gantry to facilitate the delivery of an explosive charge. The 3.Zg was a dedicated *Brückenleger-Zug* (bridge-laying platoon), equipped with a PzKpfw II and a *Brückenleger* (bridge layer) IV that was built on the chassis of a PzKpfw IV and had a load capacity of 18,000kg. However, this type could not be manufactured in the required quantities and, as a result, 20 *Brückenleger* IV b and four *Brückenleger* IV c were produced in 1940.

Far left: In 1940, a *Panzer-Pionier-Kompanie* (PzPiKp – armoured engineer company) in a PzDiv was issued with ten PzKpfw I *Sprengstoffträger* (explosive charge carrier). The type is better known as the *Ladungsleger* (load layer).

Left: An unusual conversion: The turret of this PzKpfw II Ausf b in service with a *Panzer-Ersatz-Abteilung* (PzErsAbt – training and replacement battalion) has been fitted with a jib to operate as a *Drahkran* (rotatable crane).

Bridgelaying Tanks

Production of the 8,000kg-capacity *Brückenleger* II that utilized a PzKpfw II Ausf c chassis had already begun in 1939. The two-part bridge was fabricated from steel and had an extended length of some 13m. Only a small number were, as planned, produced and three were used during the Polish campaign. After-action reports indicate that the equipment was less than useful in battle and this resulted in production being halted.

It is most certain that military planners became aware of the requirement for bridge-laying tanks to not only carry longer sections, but also have a heavier load-carrying capacity.

Before the French campaign, and with the above in mind, workshop companies in the PzDiv began to create and assemble simple but effective types by utilizing the chassis of PzKpfw I Ausf A and PzKpfw I Ausf B, as well as those of the PzKpfw II Ausf c and PzKpfw II Ausf D. The approximately 5m-long wooden bridging sections would be carried on an inclined platform fitted on the rear of an *Überbrückungswagen* (bridging vehicles). In addition, a *Pionier Übergangsschien* (engineer transition bridge) with a maximum capacity of 8,000kg was available.

An unknown number of light tanks were converted into *Uberbrückenungswagen* (bridging vehicle) and issued to mobile units to allow them to cross obstacles that could delay the advance.

A note from the HWa, dated 19 October 1939:

Bridge laying and bridging vehicles

The *Oberbefehlshaber des Heeres* [Ob d H – commander-in-chief of the army], *Generalfeldmarschall* Walter von Brauchitsch, was given an overview of the development status and production options for bridging equipment and bridging vehicles.

The Ob d H ordered:

1.) *Brückenleger* II b (Chassis PzKpfw II)

Further construction is not needed, as the main requirement is to overcome a 20m-wide obstacle.

2.) *Brückenleger* IV b (Chassis PzKpfw IV)

This type must be commissioned in larger numbers, but this depends on the availability of PzKpfw IV chassis and production capacity. The requirement is for some 20 vehicles. Delivery is required as quickly as possible, and must be given priority. The Ob d H explained that the equipment, which has not yet been tested, would not meet all requirements. Even a possible failure, as indicated by the HWa, has to be accepted. The main focus must be its use supporting trestles to cross over wide gaps.

3.) Expedient bridging vehicles

The departments involved should consult with General Guderian as to whether

A PzKpfw I Ausf B fitted with a *Pionier-Ubergangsschien* (engineers transition bridge) that had a maximum load capacity of 8,000kg.

The PzKpfw II proved to be very effective during the Polish campaign. Unfortunately, the conspicuous white *Balkenkreuz* was used as an aiming point by Polish anti-tank gunners. Consequently, tank crews often obscured them by using paint or even a coating of mud.

to make further use of the *Überbrückungswagen* and whether any further development is still required.

4.) *Überbrückungswagen* in general

Further development of new types will not be initiated because it would take too long.

The PzKpfw I *Sprengstoffträger* was issued to German units preparing for the invasion of the Low Countries and France. Here, a PzKpfw I Ausf B has the dropping device extended after delivering the 50kg explosive charge against a target.

Although the light bridge layer was little more than a carrier, unprotected crews on the battlefield found the type useful as long as it was deployed within certain parameters. Those built on the PzKpfw I chassis were probably least successful because their base vehicle was not only mechanically unreliable and time-consuming to repair, but also had very poor off-road mobility. All the units equipped with the type were ordered to remain available until the last vehicle failed or was destroyed. There would be no further development as the war progressed.

Demolition Charge Carriers

Before the start of the war, the *General der Pioniere und Festungen* (general of engineers and fortresses) demanded that mechanical devices be made available as quickly as possible to destroy obstacles such as barbed wire entanglements. His preference was for a demolition charge that would be delivered to a target by an armoured vehicle.

The *Ablegevorrichtung* (dropping device), a gantry-type frame, was fabricated from metal tubing, positioned behind the turret and attached to the superstructure of a light tank. At the end of this frame, a 50kg explosive charge protected by an armoured casing was held in place by a cable running over a pulley and into the fighting compartment. In action, the vehicle would be reversed up to the obstacle and then a crewman would release the cable, dropping the charge. A timing device prevented an immediate detonation, allowing time for the carrier to be driven to safety.

The gantry-type dropping device would have been fabricated by field engineers following drawings delivered from Germany. In action, the tank would be reversed to the target, drop the explosive charge (fitted with a time-delay fuse) and then be driven away to safety.

According to an HWa document, the PzKpfw II was initially selected for use as a *Ladungsleger* (mine carrier) vehicle and, subsequently, several vehicles were evaluated in a troop trial by PiBtl 38.

At the end of 1939, an order was issued for 100 PzKpfw II to be converted into *Panzer mit Abwurfvorrichtung* (tank with dropping device) and issued to engineer battalions in all armoured divisions; each destroyer platoon was to be issued with five vehicles.

The HWa envisaged that the repair companies in each of the divisions would fabricate the framework and complete the conversion in their own workshops from locally sourced materials. Strangely, no effort was made to manufacture a standardized conversion kit.

It has been noted that many division commanders decided, with a few exceptions, to begin by having older PzKpfw I converted into carriers. The decision was sensible, since the PzKpfw II was better armed and still regarded as an effective combat vehicle.

There are no documents available that detail the use of the demolition charge layer on the battlefront. But, on close examination of the type, its combat limitations quickly become obvious. The 50kg explosive charge was most certainly sufficient to achieve the required effect, but the problem was in delivering it to the target. The carrier had to be carefully reversed up to a target, then halt to drop the charge before speeding away to safety. The brave crewmen carried out the operation despite receiving fire from all types of enemy weapons. Although

The most common variant was fitted with a longer boom that made it safer for a crew to deliver a charge to a target. The carrying bucket was fitted with an armoured backplate to protect the charge from infantry fire. In 1941, any remaining vehicles were sent to the *Ost* (East) Front, where all were destroyed or abandoned.

the armour on a light tank was safe against 7.92mm SmK ammunition, it could be easily penetrated by an anti-tank rifle and defeated by most anti-tank guns. It can be assumed that, under these circumstances, any operations to remove reinforced roadblocks were the exception rather than the rule.

The HWa planned to fit a rotating charge-dropping device on the turret of a PzKpfw IV, but any development was not pursued.

Later in the war, un-manned remotely or radio-controlled tracked carriers were designed and manufactured to deliver a demolition charge to clear an

The PzPiBtl attached to 2.PzDiv used a small number of PzKpfw II Ausf c *Sprengstoffträger*. The rear armour was only 14.5mm thick making the vehicle vulnerable to anti-tank and heavy machine gun fire.

obstruction or a passage through a minefield. Again, these did not meet the high expectations held by the HWa.

The future belonged to armoured vehicles with heavier weapons, special types such as the *Sturmpanzer* (StuPz – assault tank) IV, known as the *Brummbär* (grizzly bear) and the *Sturmtiger* VI, armed with a 38cm *Mörser* (mortar) in German service. The British Army had the Churchill Mk III or Mk IV AVRE (Armoured Vehicle Royal Engineers), armed with a 230mm Petard spigot mortar.

Flammpanzer II

Even before the start of the Polish campaign, it was decided that the concept of the *leichte Divisionen* (leDiv – light divisions) would be abandoned, despite their good strategic mobility. This action signalled the end of PzKpfw II Ausf D production and all available vehicles were to be used for new duties. No reports have survived from the fighting in Poland that detail the mechanical reliability or battlefield performance of the type. Only two units, PzAbt [verl] 66 and PzAbt [verl] 67 were issued with the PzKpfw II Ausf D.

At the beginning of 1939, military planners decided to develop a *Flammpanzer* (flamethrower tank) based on the PzKpfw II Ausf D. The turret was removed and replaced with a much smaller type mounting an MG 34. A flamethrower was mounted on each track guard, above the drive sprocket, and both were operated from inside the vehicle. Each weapon was supplied from an armoured 160L tank of flame oil, also mounted on the track guard, that

Around 150 *Flammpanzer* (F – flame-thrower tanks) utilized the chassis of the PzKpfw II Ausf D *Schnellkampfwagen* (fast tank). Two remotely operated nozzles, mounted on the track guard above the drive sprockets, sprayed up to 80 bursts of flame up to a range of 30m.

allowed 80 bursts of flame to be delivered from up to a maximum range of 30m. By the end of 1940, 86 of the type had been completed. A further series of 65 vehicles was completed between 1941 and 1942.

In 1940, the vehicles were used to establish two *Panzerabteilung (Flamm)* (PzAbt[F] – tank battalion [flame]), the PzAbt(F) 100 and PzAbt(F) 102. In 1941, both PzAbt were first deployed during the initial phase of *Unternehmen Barbarossa*.

The type did not prove a success on the battlefield, mainly because the range of the flamethrower was too short (the later SdKfz 251/16 *Flamm-Panzerwagen* had a maximum range of 60m). Combat experience was so bad that both units were disbanded in December 1941. Consequently, all existing *Flammpanzer* were delivered to *Heereszeugämter* (army vehicle depots) and stored until 1942, when the chassis were converted to produce self-propelled anti-tank guns.

Below: Enemy gunners found the kl PzBefWg (SdKfz 265) easy to recognize due to the tall, box-like superstructure. The white cross made it even more conspicuous.

Left: Tanks of 4.PzDiv undergoing routine maintenance at a repair point during the Polish campaign. The original divisional marking, a stylized three-pointed star, was changed in early 1940. Note that the *Balkenkreuze* on all vehicles have been obscured by their crews using mud.

Below: The armour on a light tank could not withstand a hit from a heavy weapon. Here, a PzKpfw II Ausf c has been immobilized after being hit by artillery shells.

Denmark and Norway

During the occupation of Denmark and Norway as part of *Unternehmen Weserübung*, a tank unit, the *Panzer-Abteilung (zur besonderen Verwendung)* (PzAbt [zbV] – tank battalion [special duties]) 40, was established and issued with 29 PzKpfw I, 18 PzKpfw II, four PzBefWg and two NbFz medium tanks, but the latter would not be delivered until the battalion arrived in Norway.

On 17 April 1940, the detachment embarked on the German ships *Cordoba*, *Campinas* and *Wandsbeck*, and awaited orders to sail for Oslo, Norway.

On 24 April 1940, the commander of PzAbt (zbV) 40, *Oberstleutnant* Ernst Volckheim (he had commanded an A7V tank in World War I), submitted a report on the deployment in Denmark:

> The deployment brought the following experiences. The leadership of a tank formation, when its elements are spread far apart, is only possible if the commander has effective radio communications. This is mainly necessary to manage the supply of ammunition and repairs. The company assigned to *Marschgruppe* (marching group) B would remain attached to PzAbt (zbV) 40 only until it reached Tondern in Norway. The radio section tried in vain to signal the company to proceed further,

Crewmen from German tank column inspect two abandoned Polish Type 7 TP jv tanks. The type was a licence-built development of a Vickers 6-ton Mark E, that had very light armour making the tank vulnerable to fire from an anti-tank rifle or anti-tank gun.

but the commander had no direct radio connection and the company remained stationery for a few hours. The rapid advance of the other units confirms that the leadership of the battalion was only possible with the help of a car. The speed of the tanks was so great (45kph) that the commander, after receiving new orders from the division, would not have reached the troops without a car. The combat staff section was a short distance in front of the tanks. A reliable radio communication between the departmental staff and the company was not possible because of the short range of the devices and the rapid advance.

The original plan was to use only the PzKpfw I in Denmark, but it soon became evident that the PzKpfw II with the 2cm cannon was very successful. In one incident, if the company commander's tank had been a PzKpfw I, the entire crew would have died when advancing on Hadersleben [Haderslev]. However, since the officer could use a PzKpfw II with reinforced armour, they all withstood the fire from 2cm Madsen anti-tank guns (six frontal hits). As a consequence, it is not justified to use the PzKpfw I when facing enemy anti-tank units. Numerous PzKpfw I were left behind due to the high speed of the march. The many mechanical failures are due to the age of the vehicles. In operations over large areas, only tanks that are up to these tasks should be used.

The PzKpfw I are not. The battalion lacks enough suitable recovery services and repair facilities. An armoured formation that is used in large areas requires a workshop company and low-loader trailers. The assigned workshop train was not up to the task. The population in general were friendly, polite and accommodating. Everywhere there was great interest in our military vehicles and especially the tanks. Our discipline and morale were admired.

On 30 April, an unknown unit reported:

The fighting of the last few days has revealed that, contrary to previous assumptions, the enemy has concealed anti-tank weapons in houses. Here, the PzKpfw I and PzKpfw II suffered severe losses.

On 4 May 1940, a somewhat bizarre report was sent:

In the afternoon, we were ordered to put on a parade of force with our PzKpfw IV [NbFz].

The report delivered by Volckheim emphasizes just how effective the 2cm KwK 30 mounted in the PzKpfw II was, especially in the fight against infantry positioned in the mountains, where its limited elevation proved not to be a hindrance.

Fall Gelb – France

At the beginning of the western campaign, the ten German armoured divisions had significantly more tanks with higher firepower in action – 118 PzKpfw 35(t), 207 PzKpfw 38(t), 349 PzKpfw III and 280 PzKpfw IV. Nevertheless, the total number of light tanks remained high, with 554 PzKpfw I and 920 PzKpfw II. The PzKpfw I was no longer deployed for direct front-line combat and a number had been assigned to the *Panzer-Pionier-Battaillon* (PzPiBtl – armoured engineer battalion). The vehicles still available in the light companies were used for security or liaison purposes.

During Operation *Weserübung*, the invasion of Norway, PzAbt 40 (zbV) was the only tank unit to be deployed. Other than the three 7.5cm-armed NbFz prototypes, the unit was issued with light tanks. (Getty)

On 18 May 1940, the commander of PzRgt 35 (4.PzDiv), *Oberstleutnant* Heinrich Eberbach, delivered a detailed report:

Tank battle south of Hannut on 12 May 1940

Our 5.Kp, sent out to the west and southwest of Hannut, near Crehen, as security encountered 11 enemy tanks (Hotchkiss) while combing the outskirts of the village. Of these, eight were knocked out in the course of the battle, most by PzKpfw III (3.7cm KwK). The adjutant, *Oberleutnant* Einhardt Malguth, who was sent by the Abt to clarify the situation, intervened in the fight and put three more enemy tanks out of action with his 2cm KwK. It became apparent that the visibility from inside the enemy tanks was very poor. Malguth also discovered that the turret traversing on the enemy tanks was not quick enough to track a PzKpfw II being driven at

A PzKpfw Ausf A passes the wreck of an FCM 36 from a French armoured cavalry unit. The type was well armoured and could, unlike other French types in service during 1940, fight but not often defeat German armour. Like Great Britain, France had a large number of infantry tanks attached to infantry units.

speed across the battlefield.

6.Kp knocked out two enemy tanks retreating on the north-eastern edge of Hannut. Both had earlier disabled a PzKpfw IV by hitting the driver's side visor at a distance of 80m–100m.

A PzKpfw II that was fired on by an enemy tank with a 3.7cm gun [*] at 400m showed no damage on the armour. The wounded lying on the tank were not injured by small pieces of shrapnel.

Tank battle south of Hannut on 12 May 1940

An enemy tank that drove up a hill was fired on at a range of some 800m by 2cm, 3.7cm and 7.5cm KwK. A large number of hits, including some from 7.5cm KwK, were clearly observed, but the enemy was not halted by our fire and retreated back

A PzKpfw I Ausf A and a PzKpfw IV Ausf D of 2.PzDiv loaded on a railway wagon in preparation for transport to France in 1940.

Vehicles from a light tank company attached to 4.PzDiv advance through a French village. A mixed force of PzKpfw II and PzKpfw III was feared by the French infantry and dug-in artillery.

behind the hill. A little later it was found damaged, abandoned in a ravine and we discovered that it was a Somua with very heavy armour that showed numerous hit marks [**].

The report concluded with an evaluation of the light tanks:

The PzKpfw I cannot be used in tank-versus-tank combat. It must be replaced by the PzKpfw III in the PzRgt and used elsewhere. The PzKpfw II with *Panzerschürzen* [***] is to be retained as intended in the tank companies for special purposes including combat reconnaissance. If the type could be fitted with the excellent French 2.5cm anti-tank gun [this fired tungsten ammunition], it would become an effective tank, especially if visibility was improved by adding a cupola. The 2cm KwK is only effective against the Hotchkiss at a range of 200m. Unfortunately, the regiment's PzKpfw II did not receive armour skirts before deployment, and this deficiency had to be compensated for by the courage of the crews and paid for with the loss of men and material.
The French 2.5cm anti-tank gun can penetrate the armour of a PzKpfw III from a range of 500m. The French 4.7cm anti-tank gun is an excellent weapon that can penetrate the armour of a PzKpfw III even at a range of 1,500m.

[*] The 37mm SA18 L/21 mounted in the Renault R-35 only fired high-explosive rounds that were used for infantry support and were not effective against armour.

[**] The Somua S-35 was a well-balanced vehicle with respectable armour (40mm to 47mm) and an effective 47mm SA35 L/32 gun.

[***] In this context, the term 'armoured apron' refers to the 20mm additional armour on the bow plate, on the front of the driver's position and the front of the turret.

Czechoslovak-built Tanks

At the beginning of the French campaign, more than 200 PzKpfw 38(t) were available. These were assigned to the PzRgt 25 and PzAbt noted, the type effectively filled the role of the PzKpfw III due to its armour-piercing weapon.

From a report delivered by 7.PzDiv:

> The German tanks [PzKpfw38(t)] have effective armament and good optics. In this respect, it appears to be superior to both the French and British armour. The division also has the impression that the German tank is faster than those of the enemy. But perhaps this conclusion is only drawn from the fact that these attacks were carried out at the highest possible speed (*). The chassis of the PzKpfw 38(t) has proven to be good and durable and is superior to all German types in this

All the 3.7cm-armed PzKpfw 35(t) issued to 6.PzDiv were deployed as *Kampfwagen* (battle tanks). Here, an entire company has been deployed and supported by *Schützen-Abteilung* (rifle battalion).

From 1940, all PzKpfw II were fitted with 20mm of additional armour on the front plate and turret front. However, the measure only gave protection from anti-tank and heavy machine guns.

respect. The number of PzKpfw 38(t) failing mechanically on three consecutive day marches, each some 280km, was insignificant.

A note on the effectiveness of enemy weapons is interesting:

The 2.5cm and 4.7cm anti-tank guns deployed by the enemy were particularly effective. Both weapons are superior to our 3.7cm PaK in terms of rate of fire and penetration. The frequent use of the 7.5cm cannon was found to be particularly effective [**]. These were often well camouflaged and set up at roadblocks; the enemy usually opened fire at 50m range, frequently having a devastating effect on our tanks and armoured reconnaissance vehicles.

[*] The commander of 7.PzDiv, *Generalmajor* Erwin Rommel, was well known, and somewhat notorious, for his tendency to carry out long-distance attacks on his own without instructions from superior authorities. He also showed little regard for having flank cover, any supply services or the support of other German units. The unpredictability and speed of his operations irritated not only his opponents, but also the German high command. This caused his

Above: Although considered to be obsolete, the light tank could still be used to protect rear areas as the main force continued the advance. On many occasions, they would be deployed to mop up scattered enemy units or to protect engineer bridges.

Left: The superstructure on this kl PzBefWg, in service with the regimental staff of 3.PzDiv, has been hit by a shell, possibly from a Red Army 7.62mm artillery gun, and ripped open.

division to become known as the *Gespensterdivision* (Ghost Division).

[**] The 75mm *Canon de 75 modéle* 1897 was issued to French units at divisional level as a field gun that was also effective in anti-tank defence.

On 30 May 1940, PzRgt 25 reported:

> The 7.PzDiv had destroyed 18 heavy and 295 light tanks by the above date, of which six heavy and 171 light tanks were directly engaging PzRgt 25. The regiment lost 20 PzKpfw 35(t), four PzKpfw IV, nine PzKpfw II and ten PzKpfw I in the battle.

In 1940, only one unit, 6.PzDiv, had been issued with the PzKpfw 35(t), having received 116 of the type along with 60 PzKpfw II, 23 PzKpfw IV and 15 command vehicles.

Light tanks of 4.PzDiv have taken up their starting positions for the attack. After Poland, military planners decided that all armoured vehicles were to be fitted with *Nebelkurzenab-wurfvorrichtung* (NKAV – smoke grenade launchers).

Out of range to enemy artillery, elements of a PzDiv prepare to advance. The commander of the PzKpfw II wears *Doppel-Fernhöhrer* (Dfh – headphones) to listen to radio traffic. The tank has been fitted with additional 20mm armour on the bow and front plate, also on the front of the turret.

Waterways represent an effective obstacle to an advancing force. Here, a PzKpfw II from the regimental staff of 7.PzDiv crosses a canal using a pontoon bridge assembled by the attached PzPiBtl.

Tanks from 7.PzDiv, commanded by Erwin Rommel, parked in the narrow confines of a French village. Note a 7.62mm *Maschinenpistole* (MP – submachine gun) 18, the first of the type to be issued to German troops, has been leant against the turret front of this PzKpfw II.

After the end of the campaign, the commander of the division answered some questions from a superior command level:

> How did our armoured fighting vehicles prove themselves and against what weapons of the enemy did they not offer security?
>
> Our PzKpfw generally performed very well. The gun optics of the PzKpfw 35(t) are inadequate, as are the vision devices for both commander and driver. The armour, especially the frontal armour, is insufficient. It does not even protect against the French 2.5cm anti-tank gun. The armour of a battle tank should be of similar thickness as that of our StuG [*], which proved to be immune. However, the stronger armour should not compromise cross-country mobility or marching speed. The British 7.5cm gun, widely used in concealed firing position for direct fire, proved to be an excellent and mobile weapon, and was effective for anti-tank combat [**]. The French 2.5cm and 4.7cm anti-tank guns could penetrate our tanks, and that indicates that our vehicles have inadequate armour. The French 7.5cm gun was judged similarly to the British gun.

[*] At times, 6.PzDiv had an attached *Sturmbatterie* (assault battery) with six *Sturmgeschütz* (StuG – assault guns).

[**] Almost all combatants used 7.5cm field guns at divisional level. Germany, on the other hand, decided to introduce the 10.5cm le FH 18, but the weapon was almost impossible to use for direct fire and was difficult to move.

Above: After the fall of France, German forces that remained began a series of amphibious landing exercises as preparations for *Unternehmen Seelöwe* (Operation Sea Lion) the planned invasion of Great Britain. The PzKpfw I is in service with PzJgAbt 643 as a command vehicle.

Production Improvements

Production of the PzKpfw II was temporarily halted in April 1940, to rectify a number of faults and weak points that became apparent after the type had entered front-line service. An important improvement was the fitting of a low-profile cupola, with vision blocks, for the commander and the driver now had an armour-protected vision device.

After the end of the Polish campaign, the tank crews continued to complain about the lack of armour protection, since Polish anti-tank rifles and anti-tank guns could penetrate 14.5mm plate at virtually any range.

To keep the weight of the tank within specified limits, only the armour on frontal areas – the bow, front plate and turret – could be reinforced. As a result, the manufactures began producing 20mm-thick protection plates that were to be fitted during production or at a vehicle depot or by a workshop unit in the field. The PzKpfw now had 35mm, but this would soon be rendered insufficient as the enemy introduced more powerful anti-tank guns into service. In a contest between anti-tank weaponry and the armour on a light tank, the latter would never win.

The PzKpfw II Ausf D was designed as a fast combat vehicle, and as a result, it was fitted Christie-type torsion bar suspension. Interior space was enlarged by repositioning the fuel tank in the engine compartment.

Balkans Deployment

In March 1941, the *Panzertruppe* decided to initiate a phase of reorganization by equipping le PzKp with PzKpfw III (17 tanks) and m PzKp with PzKpfw IV (14 tanks). Five PzKpfw II were issued only to the *leichte Zug* (le Zg – light platoon) in each company. Light tank platoons at battalion and regimental staff level were each issued with five PzKpfw II.

Although seen as ideal, the actual assembly could only be carried out gradually – for instance, the number of PzKpfw III available was still too small, causing each division to adapt the new organization as tanks became available. Also, the staff companies of many armoured divisions were only assigned PzKpfw II and PzBefWg.

On 6 April 1941, German units launched *Unternehmen Marita* and crossed into Yugoslavia and then Greece. This invasion became necessary due to political developments that caused Adolf Hitler to fear that his plans for an attack on the Soviet Union would be jeopardized by the presence of British troops.

Four pontoons have been joined together to create a ferry with a load capacity of 20,000kg. It is powered by two large outboard engines.

The short-lived campaign was, in the main, successful. A total of 18 PzKpfw I were divided between the six armoured divisions deployed and most were used for support duties. Also, 260 PzKpfw II were available to the divisions.

Much of the fighting took place over rock-strewn, mountainous terrain that caused many tanks to fail mechanically. In particular, the extremely delicate

Many of the PzKpfw II in service on the Eastern Front were re-assigned to *leichte Zug* (le Zg – light platoons) at regimental or battalion HQ level, where they would be used for security or reconnaissance duties. The motorcycle-mounted *Kradmelder* (dispatch rider) was often the only reliable means of communication on the battlefront.

final drive units, drive sprockets and leaf springs failed with some frequency. The most serious problem was with the rubber tyres on the running wheels, which disintegrated after a very short time in use. However, the campaign showed that the tank could, despite the obvious problems, be of use in such an environment.

Right: A PzKpfw II from the regimental staff of an unknown PzDiv passes the vehicles and equipment used by men of the PzPiBtl to construct a bridge.

A number of PzKpfw I or PzKpfw II *Sprengstoffträger* were available to PzPioBn when *Unternehmen Barbarossa* was launched on 22 June 1941, and German forces invaded the Soviet Union. But Red Army anti-tank troops had been issued with the 14.5mm PTRD heavy anti-tank rifle that could defeat both types.

North Africa

In early 1941, Hitler felt compelled to intervene in North Africa on behalf of his ally, Mussolini. In the course of Operation *Compass*, the British were able to push back the initially successful Italian forces. In early March, a small German contingent led by Rommel landed in Tripoli, a decision that some military planners viewed as a serious threat to the plan for the invasion of the Soviet Union in June 1941.

First 5.le Div and, a little later, the 15.PzDiv arrived in North Africa and had a combined force of some 25 PzKpfw I and 90 PzKpfw II, along with 142 PzKpfw III armed with a 5cm KwK L/42 and 40 PzKpfw IV armed with the 7.5cm KwK L/24.

The climate of North Africa caused a number of modifications to be implemented to make the vehicles suitable for use in desert conditions.

From March 1941, field engineers began work on the first of various *Formänderungen* (detailed modifications). In order to improve engine cooling, all tanks, including the PzKpfw I and PzKpfw II, were fitted with high-performance

fans and also enlarged ducts for the ingress of cooling air. Engine access covers were replaced by a new type that had ventilation louvres. The original fuel filters easily became clogged with dust and were replaced with a more effective *Filzbalzfilter* (bellows-type filter).

Again, the rubber tyres on running wheels on both the PzKpfw I and PzKpfw II would frequently be destroyed by a combination of heat and the terrain. Consequently, the spare part stores attempted to keep a large reserve of these in stock, but there were frequent shortages. During rest periods,

This trench crossing was built using planks that had been carried into position on a PzKpfw II from 15.PzDivi.

crews were told to cover the running the wheels to protect them from the intense heat.

The PzKpfw I was of little use in the wide, open spaces of the North African desert, and if an enemy force was encountered, it would be knocked out before its machine guns could be brought into firing range.

Of the original 25 PzKpfw I delivered, none remained in service after a year, nor were any listed in the equipment tables produced in May 1942. Neither the PzKpfw 35(t) nor the PzKpfw 38(t) went to Libya.

PzKpfw II from 5.PzDiv lined up for inspection
on Martyrs' Square after being landed in Tripoli.
The tank crews are wearing the distinctive
Panzerwaffe black overalls.

PzKpfw II Ausf F

In March 1941, production began of the PzKpfw II Ausf F, although the order had been issued in 1939. The type was fitted with leaf-spring suspension and running gear, as used for the PzKpfw II Ausf c. The frontal armour was increased to 35mm and an improved commander's dome, with seven vision devices, was fitted. Production of the PzKpfw Ausf F ended in mid-1942, after some 500 had been completed.

The Opponent

From the end of 1941, the British armed forces began to receive the US-built Light Tank M3. Adapted to British requirements and known as the Stuart Mk1 to MkV, this tank was in some respects comparable with the PzKpfw II.

According to its mechanical and performance data, the Stuart was clearly superior to the PzKpfw II, despite being significantly heavier (14,200kg). The type was of riveted construction and had armour equalling that of the PzKpfw III. This meant that, by 1942, the Stuart, unlike the PzKpfw II, could also be used for tank-versus-tank combat. Fighting the type with the 2cm KwK,

A PzKpfw II Ausf F, the final variant that was produced in 1942, next to a PzKpfw IV. Both vehicles have been carefully camouflaged in a cactus grove, vital for survival in the open terrain of the North African desert.

A PzKpfw I Ausf A, from the staff section of 5.le Div, being loaded onto a transport ship in Naples. This division was formed from elements of 3.PzDiv and continued to use the same markings. In August 1941, 5.le Div was converted to a standard PzDiv and renamed the 21.PzDiv.

mounted in the PzKpfw II, was usually unsuccessful, but the German 5cm KwK L/60, mounted in the PzKpfw III Ausf M, could defeat a Stuart at up to 1,000m range.

The PzKpfw III, armed with a 5cm KwK L/60, was the most important tank in the inventory of the *Panzerarmee Afrika* until the arrival of the PzKpfw IV Ausf G, mounting a 7.5cm KwK L/43.

The Stuart was armed with a 37mm Gun M5 or M6, firing armour-piercing ammunition to fight enemy tanks or high-explosive (HE) ammunition to destroy infantry positions. The type could also be armed with up to five 0.30in M1919 machine guns.

As a light tank, the (M3) Stuart was far more versatile than the PzKpfw II by having a significantly higher speed, ideal for a fast attack or battlefront reconnaissance missions.

The type was fitted with Vertical-Volute Suspension System (VVSS) running gear that was mechanically more robust and reliable than the suspension on the PzKpfw II. Production ended in September 1943, after some 13,859 had been completed, of which 5,473 – although a document in the library at the Tank Museum, Bovington, UK, states 6,582 – were delivered to the British Army. The Red Army received 3,012 under the Lend-Lease Program.

The M3A3 was succeeded by the Light Tank M5A1 that entered production in April 1942, and of the 6,810 completed ,1,131 were delivered to the British Army as the Stuart Mk VI. Interestingly, both types were being produced in parallel until September 1943.

PzKpfw II Ausf F

Year:	1941–1942
Weight:	9,500kg
Crew:	Three
Armament:	One 2cm KwK 30; one 7.92mm MG 34
Armour:	14.5mm–35mm
Engine:	140hp Maybach HL 62 TR: six-cylinder, water-cooled
Range (maximum):	190km
Speed (maximum):	40kph

Stuart Mk I to V

Year:	1941–1943
Weight:	14,700kg
Crew:	Four
Armament:	One 37mm Gun M5 or M6; up to five 0.30in M1919 MG
Armour:	13mm–51mm
Engine:	Continental W670-9A: seven-cylinder, radial, air-cooled
	Guiberson T-1020-4 nine-cylinder, radial, air-cooled (diesel) [*]
Range (maximum):	120km
Speed (maximum):	58kph

[*] 1,285 entered British service as the Stuart Mk II.

A PzKpfw II Ausf F of 5.le Div after unloading in the port of Tripoli. The searing heat on the North African battlefront caused serious damage to the rubber tyres fitted on the running wheels.

The Invasion of Russia

When *Unternehmen Barbarossa* was launched on 22 June 1941, the *Wehrmacht* deployed a combined force of some 3,000 tanks and self-propelled guns, including a significant number of light tanks – 152 PzKpfw I and 743 PzKpfw II. A total of 1,250 battle tanks were involved in the attack, of which 700 were PzKpfw III, mounting a 5cm KwK L/42, and 449 were PzKpfw IV armed with a 7.5cm KwK L/24. It is thought that, on the day of the invasion, the Red Army had some 23,000 tanks of various types at its disposal.

The light tanks were used in accordance with the experience gained in earlier battles. The PzKpfw I were mainly assigned to the PzPiBtl and used as carrier vehicles for bridging equipment and also as *Sprengstoffträger*. Where they still existed at the end of 1941, these old vehicles were used for a wide variety of tasks. Many were made available to the *Panzerjäger* (PzJg – anti-tank) units in a division as command vehicles or as a *Munitionspanzerwagen* (armoured ammunition carrier).

The PzKpfw II were assigned to the le Zg in the tank companies, and also to battalion and regimental staff companies; five tanks for each le Zg.

In January 1941, *Oberstleutnant* Wilhelm Hochbaum, commander of PzRgt 35 (4.PzDiv), delivered a report:

> A basic distinction must be made between operational reconnaissance tanks with a long range and those for tank-versus-tank operations on the battlefront. The PzKpfw II is considered ideal for battlefield reconnaissance. However, we have to note that this tank, which proved to be a mechanically robust and reliable vehicle in past campaigns, has become nose-heavy due to the application of extra armour. As a direct result, the steering brakes, transmission and engines become overloaded. The battle value of the PzKpfw II has clearly deteriorated because of this and it has become less mobile and less reliable.
>
> The PzKpfw I in the PzPiBtl are expendable because they are outdated and unreliable, and they also burden the repair services and supply lines.

Summer 1941: A PzKpfw 35(t) from 6.PzDiv in the northern sector of the Eastern Front. After the conversion, the vehicle could now carry a crew of four, although space remained cramped. This forced the crew to stow their belongings on the outside of the vehicle.

A PzKpfw 38(t) ploughs through impassable terrain of the Soviet *Rasputitsa* (mud season). The large amount of mud that accumulated in the running gear would force a driver to reduce speed, but this increased fuel consumption.

Right: A PzKpfw 35(t) ploughs across a field of wheat stubble. Note the fascine (bundle of sticks) on the rear of the tank. This would be used to form what tank crews called a *Cordstrasse* (corduroy road) to cross marshy ground.

Below: This PzKpfw 35(t) received a hit in the engine compartment that then punctured the fuel tank, causing an explosion that has destroyed the tank.

The armoured engineer company will receive two platoons of armoured personnel carriers [SdKfz 251/7] in future. These are used for clearing minefields, reconnaissance, demolition tasks and for constructing small temporary crossings. The company should also have two platoons of *Flammpanzer* to combat infantry positioned in bunkers. For this purpose, those PzKpfw II remaining in service with our m PzKp can be used, since they are expendable.

The regiment should also receive a reconnaissance company, since both the PzKpfw II and PzKpfw III are too slow, lack sufficient range and are far too noisy.

It is clear that Hochbaum did not consider that both the PzKpfw I and PzKpfw II had any value on the battlefield and were to be issued to the light platoons and the staff sections of PzAbt and PzRgt. Here they could be used as required for various duties, including as armoured transport vehicles for ammunition and fuel.

Most of the *Erfahrungsberichte* (after-action report) written at the time when the Red Army began deploying more powerful tanks were delivered by an officer or the commander of a PzKpfw III or PzKpfw IV-equipped unit.

A PzKpfw 35(t) in service with 6.PzDiv is followed by a PzKpfw I that has been converted for use as an ammunition or supplies carrier. Interestingly, a number were used as recovery tractors by field engineers.

Below: The driver of this PzKpfw 35(t) has been unable to reverse his vehicle out of this steep-sided ditch. The task will pass to the recovery services to retrieve the vehicle.

The crew of a PzKpfw 35(t) inspect the wreck of a Red Army BT-7 light tank. Although very different, both were similarly effective on the battlefield, but superior German combat tactics often made the difference.

In October 1941, the commander of 4.PzDiv, *Generalmajor* Willibald Freiherr von Langermann und Erlencamp, delivered a report:

To combat the Soviet tank threat, I respectfully propose the following:

a.) All captured Soviet T-34 medium and KV-1 heavy tanks, whenever feasible, must be immediately refurbished and issued to our units.

b.) Install the Soviet 76.2mm field gun [ZiS-3] in the PzKpfw IV, if necessary, without a *Panzerführer* and the extra armour; the MG could also be omitted.

c.) Production of a self-propelled 10cm PzJg [*] with minimum of six issued to each PzRgt.

d.) Urgent development of significantly more powerful and effective anti-tank ammunition.

e.) As an immediate measure, installation of a 5cm PaK in the PzKpfw III, even if this makes the vehicle top-heavy.

[*]   10cm s K18 PzSfl IVa known as *Dicker* (fat) Max.

The HWa had already taken action in early 1942 by ordering the installation of the 5cm KwK L/60 in the PzKpfw III, and the 7.5cm KwK 40 L/43 in the PzKpfw IV.

These statements confirm the absolute superiority of the armour and armament of the latest T-34 medium and KV-1 heavy tanks over the opposing PzKpfw III and PzKpfw IV.

PzKpfw 35(t)

In June 1941, 6.PzDiv, issued with 47 PzKpfw II, 155 PzKpfw 35(t), 30 PzKpfw IV and 13 PzBeflWg, was in the vanguard of the German invasion forces that had crossed into Soviet territory. It soon became clear that the 3.7cm gun lacked sufficient ballistic performance to defeat the new types of medium and heavy tanks being deployed by the Red Army.

Despite this, the German advance continued apace, but there were a number of serious defeats resulting from a lack of firepower. Nevertheless, the *Wehrmacht* continued to operate as a cohesive force, supported by the *Luftwaffe,* and arrived at the gates of Moscow on 20 October 1941.

The available war diaries of 6.PzDiv reveal some major problems. The 3.7cm KwK mounted in the PzKpfw 35(t) could immobilize a T-34 with a hit to the tracks or optics, but lacked the power to penetrate the armour. To overcome the problem, the division deployed their m PzKp, issued with PzKpfw IV armed with a 7.5cm KwK L/24, to front any tank-versus-tank battle.

Armoured command vehicles were also produced by utilizing a PzKpfw 35(t) chassis. The front machine gun had to be removed (the hole was covered with a plate) to create the space required for the additional radio equipment.

A PzKpfw 38(t) in service with PzRgt 25 attached to 7.PzDiv. The regiment had 12 PzKp, as indicated by the unusual four-digit turret number.

The weapon fired armour-piercing ammunition that could, at very short range, jam the turret of enemy tanks or destroy its tracks and running gear.

Interestingly, the anti-tank units in 6.PzDiv were issued with the 5cm PaK 38 that also, despite firing the PzGr 40, could not penetrate the armour on the T-34 and KV-1.

As a result, the PzKpfw 35(t) were only to be used offensively against the older types that the Red Army continued to deploy in large numbers. Here, superior German combat tactics, along with radio equipment and good observation devices, allowed tank commanders to fight with some success.

Whenever a force of T-34 and KV-1 appeared, battle groups formed of PzKpfw IV and PzKpfw II would be deployed and, when available, supported by 8.8cm anti-aircraft guns.

A battle report from 20 July 1941, illustrates the severity of the fighting:

Report on the use of the 2./PzPiBtl 57 against a Red Army advance along the road north of Leshgolovo.
On 19 July, 2./PzPiBtl 57 had moved into woodland west of the advance road near Sargoye. The company had the task of holding the road and the bridges over the

Light bridges assembled by PzPiBtl were often restricted for use by wheeled vehicles. A shallow river could easily be crossed by a PzKpfw 38(t) and other types with a similar fording capability.

Dolgaja, Werza and Luga, as well as securing the advance road and another bridge to the west. Contact had been established with 3./SchtzRgt 114 in Paoserje and the FlaK unit positioned at the church in Paoserje. On the evening of 19 July, at around 23:00hrs, Soviet bombers attacked and a direct hit on the company left four dead, 11 wounded and 20 slightly wounded. When Red Army reconnaissance troops attempted to cross the Dolgaja at around 05:00hrs, they were fired on by defending troops and forced to retreat. They then took up positions on the river bank. The enemy then used heavy artillery and mortar fire to pound our positions on the edge of the forest, before their infantry, approximately battalion-sized, began to advance towards the bridge over the Dolgaya. As a result, we requested that the FlaK unit open fire, and this caused the enemy to abandon his plan and retreat back into the woods. A PzKpfw IV, a PzKpfw II of the PzRgt and two armoured personnel carriers tried to assault the enemy on his left flank, but this failed. Unfortunately, we lost two tanks and an armoured personnel carrier to artillery fire. The Soviets launched another attack from a distance of 250m, which we repelled after the enemy had lost a significant number of troops. At this point, our company almost ran out of ammunition.

The PzKpfw 35(t) was, in many respects, a modern tank, fitted with some advanced features – the gear change, brakes and steering were pneumatically (air pressure) operated, which lessened the driver's workload by making the vehicle extraordinarily smooth to operate. This, along with an advanced type of suspension and running gear, was appreciated during peacetime military exercises, but reality struck when the PzKpfw 35(t) was deployed for *Unternehmen Barbarossa*.

Here, the type reached its limits. Firstly, the onset of *Rasputitsa* (mud season) caused problems with the small running wheels and complex external leaf springs of the running gear, which became clogged with the heavy, sticky mud. When the latter froze, the problems multiplied as track links and leaf springs fractured in the intense cold.

However, the most serious problem was with the pneumatic operating system. With the onset of the harsh Soviet winter, any condensation in the system would freeze and prevent the vehicle from being driven. The problem could only be rectified by the vehicle being taken to a workshop unit for specialist repair.

The SdAnh 115 had sufficient load-carrying capacity to recover a PzKpfw 38(t). Here, the trailer is being towed by an SdKfz 8 heavy half-track tractor. Both vehicles have been camouflaged with a coating of whitewash paint.

In December 1941, 6.PzDiv was transferred from HG *Nord* to HG *Mitte*, which was holding positions near the centre of Moscow. By January 1942, after weeks of hand-to-hand fighting, the virtually annihilated division was pulled out of the battle. In March 1942, what remained of the division was transferred to France to be rested and then re-equipped, ready for action by November 1942. The PzKpfw 35(t) was declared obsolete and those vehicles that remained were to be used for training or as armoured tractors.

PzKpfw 38(t)

During the attack on the Soviet Union in June 1941, the *Wehrmacht* had 17 armoured divisions at its disposal and five – 7.PzDiv, 8.PzDiv, 12.PzDiv,

This PzKpfw II has received a direct hit on the turret ring, hurling the entire assembly off the hull. In the background is a French-built Laffly V15 T light artillery tractor that had been captured after the fall of France. Both are in service with 8.PzDiv, but the Laffly is from the recovery section.

19.PzDiv and 20.PzDiv – were issued with the PzKpfw 38(t). By including the PzKpfw 35(t) issued to 6.PzDiv, more than a third of the offensive units involved were equipped with 3.7cm KwK-armed fighting vehicles. This confirms just how important the Czechoslovak-built tanks were to the German war machine – and the fact that a large part of the German tank force was equipped with types completely unable to defeat tanks such as the T-34 and KV-1.

However, the PzKpfw 38(t) and, to a certain extent, the PzKpfw 35(t) were considered by their crews to have excellent mobility and, in general, to be very reliable. Workshop units found that both types were straightforward to maintain. But the lack firepower, even when firing armour-piercing ammunition,

Men from a *Werkstatt-Kompanie* (workshop company) replace both final drive units on a PzKpfw II. These complicated and delicate units failed with some regularity due to mechanical problems that were never solved.

meant that a commander had to always be aware of an opponent's weaponry.

When Germany launched its summer offensive in spring 1942, three divisions – 8.PzDiv, 19.PzDiv and 22.PzDiv – were still mostly equipped with the PzKpfw 38(t).

The use of the latter, which was intended to fulfil the role of a medium tank, was problematic.

A field commander in PzRgt 204 (22.PzDiv), who witnessed the fighting that led to the breakthrough at Parpatsch, reported:

Battle report for the attack on 20 March 1942 at Korpetsch:

The approach by the regiment from the Stary Krim area to the fruit plantation area south of Bairatsch was uneventful.

At 05:00hrs, I gave the order to line up. I.Abt started, but the *Schützen-panzerwagen* [SPW – armoured half-track carrier] company came to a halt and that delayed the start of II.Abt. As a result, the gap between the two battalions was too large and prevented a direct line of attack. The first 1,000m–1,500m to the holding position was covered at low speed because of poor visibility. I then ordered a halt at 05:15hrs until 05:30hrs, but the visibility did not improve. Elements of the rifle brigade reached the regiment coming from the south. A brief discussion ensued between the regiment commander and the commander of I.Abt. At 05:30hrs, I ordered them to start. At first, PzRgt drove cautiously, then increased speed and surprised the enemy who abandoned their positions. On the way, the connection between the two battalions was lost due to the weather. At 05:55hrs, I.Abt encountered Red Army tanks south of Tulumchak, including the heaviest of the KV type. Our PzKpfw 38(t) were withdrawn immediately. Although our PzKpfw IV were ordered to advance, they were forced to retreat after a number had been knocked out.

At 06.21hrs, I.Abt requested help from PzArtRgt and the division ordered them to bring a battery forward to engage the enemy tanks by direct fire. Although the Red Army heavy tanks were halted, I.Abt had suffered considerable losses in the fighting. At 06.45hrs, the commander left with II.Abt and the attached SPW company. The tanks were being delayed in the swampy area around the small stream, but elements of the heavy company did manage to reach Height 28.2 at Korpetsch. The enemy artillery then opened fire to cover an attack by their heavy tanks that knocked out two PzKpfw IV and seriously damaged several other tanks. Consequently, Height 28.2 could not be held, since the main part of II.Abt remained under heavy artillery fire, having been halted in the sodden terrain. The majority of the tanks lost by II.Abt were stopped by heavy artillery fire while attempting to find crossing places to the north and south of Korpetsch. The 3./PiBtl 28, which was attached to the division and had the task of erecting crossings, could not get to the stream due to the heavy fire, and was also stranded on the right flank of the rifle brigade positioned halfway to Korpetsch.

The 20.PzDiv was issued with PzKpfw 38(t) until the end of 1942. When the division was re-equipped, a number of the type were retained and converted to carry a Bilstein manually operated crane. Here, the main gun, a 7.5cm KwK L/43, is being removed from the turret of a PzKpfw IV Ausf G.

The division analyzed the reasons why this attack failed:

- The enemy was strong and could strike from well-prepared positions.
- The enemy had a good view over the treeless terrain.
- The attack was hampered by a narrow stream that flowed through a depression.
- The necessary pioneer forces could not be made available.
- Both the attack and all attempts to cross the stream were thwarted by enemy artillery strikes.
- Due to the special circumstances, our rear services, including the supply troops, had to be parked far to the west, out of range to enemy artillery. Camouflage was impossible.
- Our tanks were far inferior to those of the enemy, the promised PzKpfw IV (*lang*) having yet to be delivered. This meant our PzKpfw 38(t) were deployed to fight Soviet T-34 and KV-1 tanks.

The PzKpfw 38(t) of 12.PzDiv were equipped with an unusual type of smoke grenade launcher. Their turret identifiers, a letter and two numerals, were coloured yellow.

Men of the PzPiBtl in a PzDiv were virtually in constant demand as German forces continued their advance over the Eastern Front. Here, a Red Army anti-tank ditch has been filled and reinforced with wooden planks to enable vehicles, here a PzKpfw 38(t), to cross.

Self-propelled Artillery 6

Modern light tanks are often designed to have a multi-purpose role, but in World War II this was frequently not the case. Vociferous demands made by front-line troops, who were desperate for their artillery and anti-tanks to have better protection and be more mobile, caused military planners to improvise by utilizing the chassis of a current type.

The option of designing and developing a purpose-built light tank was not available to the founders of the German tank force. The PzKpfw I was initially proposed as an economically manufacturable vehicle with which to equip the planned large formations. The PzKpfw II was ordered for production due to the delay in producing the Pzkpfw III and Pzkpfw IV.

As a result, both early types were deployed on the battlefront at the beginning of the war to fight enemy light armour, dug-in infantry or for reconnaissance duties. Later, they were also to be used as command vehicles and demolition charge and equipment carriers for pioneer units.

The notion to utilize soft-skinned or armoured tracked vehicles, or only the chassis, as carriers for support weapons had been discussed at high level during the development phase of the *Panzerwaffe*. However, senior officers had already decided that priority was to be given to the formation of a large and effective tank force.

Development

At the beginning of 1940, after being pressurized by battle-hardened field commanders, officials at the HWa ordered the development of a self-propelled gun to be expedited.

The PzKpfw I was selected as being ideal for conversion, and although production had ended, a significant number were available. The Alkett company, which had already developed the StuG, was contracted to carry out the work.

Opposite: From 1942, effective anti-tank guns became available as part of the *schwere-Panzerabwehrkanone* (s PaK – heavy anti-tank gun) programme. The chassis of light tanks were used to produce self-propelled guns. The *Marder* (marten) II combined the 7.5cm PaK 40 with the chassis of the PzKpfw II.

In 1940, an order was issued to provide the *Schützen-Regimenter* (rifle regiments) in each PzDiv with mobile support artillery. As a result, 38 PzKpfw I Ausf B were adapted to carry a 15cm *schwere Infanterie-Geschütz* (sIG – heavy infantry gun) 33, including the entire carriage, by removing the turret and replacing it with a simple armoured gun shield.

Panzerjäger

In the late 1930s, German intelligence services began reporting that French tank units were beginning to receive well-armoured, difficult-to-defeat tanks. In 1940, the German tank destroyer force was only equipped with the 3.7cm PaK, a weapon that was already considered inadequate, and although the development of a better weapon – the 5cm PaK 38 – had begun, it would not be available in time for the attack on France.

In this situation, the Škoda-built 4.7cm *Kanón Proti Utočine Vozbé vzor* (KPUVvz – anti-tank gun model) 38 – 4.7cm PaK(t) or 4.7cm PaK 38(t) in German service – was selected for mounting on the chassis of a PzKpfw I Ausf B. The conversion was completed relatively easily by removing the turret and fabricating a frame over the fighting compartment to support the gun mounting. The gun and its crew were protected by a rudimentary gun shield, open at the top and rear. These simple tank destroyers were held on army troop level and attached to other units as required.

Delivery of the 5cm PaK 38 L/60 began in late 1940, and was still in progress when German forces invaded the Soviet Union in the summer of 1941. Unfortunately, when the Red Army began to deploy increasing numbers of T-34 medium and KV-1 heavy tanks, the weapon soon proved to be obsolete.

As part of the preparations for *Fall Gelb*, five PzDiv each received a battery of six 15cm sIG 33 on PzKpfw I Ausf B. The self-propelled guns performed surprisingly well, despite the type being mechanically overloaded.

Right: In 1939, German military planners were aware that the French had a number of heavily armoured tanks in service, and so they urgently sought to produce a mobile heavy anti-tank gun. This resulted in the 4.7cm PaK(t) on PzKpfw I Ausf B, which was issued at army troop level for the invasion of France.

Right: The crew of the self-propelled gun was inadequately protected due to the open three-sided superstructure being fabricated from 14.5mm steel. Despite this, the type proved to be effective on the battlefield in France.

The *Panzerjäger* (PzJg – tank hunter) I, here in service with
PzJgAbt 521, provided little space for the crew of three. All
personal belongings had to be stowed on the superstructure. By
1941, the age of the chassis led to many mechanical failures.

In the initial phase of the attack on the Soviet Union, large numbers of 76.2mm field guns were captured from the Red Army. German engineers slightly modified the powerful weapon before it was issued to artillery units. The gun was designated 7.62cm FK(r) (*russiche* – Russian origin) and used to arm self-propelled guns. Here, it is mounted on the chassis of a PzKpfw II Ausf D.

At the beginning of 1942, the 7.5cm PaK 40 L/46, an effective anti-tank weapon, was finally issued to front-line units. Also, German forces had captured a significant number of 7.62cm field guns and ammunition from the Red Army. Officials at the HWa had become aware of the advantages a self-propelled anti-tank gun had over the conventionally towed type, especially on the challenging Soviet battlefront. As a result, the organization immediately issued orders for both types of weapon to be mounted on an available tank chassis as a self-propelled gun. Initially, a number of obsolete PzKpfw II flamethrower tanks were selected for conversion, but later PzKpfw II chassis and that of the the PzKpfw 38(t) were delivered from the production line.

The production of *Selbstfahrlafette* (Sf – self-propelled) guns mounting the 7.5cm PaK 40 or 7.62cm PaK 36(r) provided German forces with an effective and highly mobile anti-tank (and conventional) artillery that often played a vital role in battle. By 1945, Germany had built some 2,500 self-propelled anti-tank guns by utilizing the chassis of light tanks.

Above: The chassis of the PzKpfw 38(t) was also utilized to carry a 7.62cm FK(r). The new *Selbstfahrlafette* (Sfl - self-propelled) anti-tank guns were assigned to tank destroyer units attached to Panzer and infantry divisions.

Left: A 7.5cm PaK 40 auf PzKpfw II (*Marder* II) being loaded into an Me 323 transport aircraft. The heavy machine enabled strategic air transport within ranges of up to 1,100km.

The 7.5cm and 7.62cm-armed self-propelled anti-tank guns gave tank destroyer units the firepower required to defeat Red Army T-34 medium and KV heavy tanks. The crew, however, had little protection from the weather, enemy infantry fire or shrapnel from exploding shells.

Right: Spring 1943: An Ausf H *Marder* III, in service with 1.SS-PzDiv Leibstandarte Adolf Hitler, in a suburban area of Kharkov. When deployed in a built-up area, the vehicle would always be supported by *Panzergrenadier* (PzGren – armoured infantry).

Below: The PzKpfw II chassis could carry the weight of an anti-tank gun and superstructure and still perform well.

Support Artillery

As the invasion of Poland progressed, it became apparent to field commanders that a PzDiv lacked firepower, particularly in the critical phase of an attack. Slowly, the concept of combined arms combat began to be appreciated.

At the beginning of the war, the artillery assigned to infantry and armoured divisions was issued with weapons of different calibres and ballistic capabilities:

- 7.5cm *leichtes Infanteriegeschütz* (le IG – light infantry gun) 18
- 15cm *schweres Infanteriegeschütz* (s IG – heavy infantry gun) 33

The artillery regiment in a division was issued with flat- and high-trajectory guns, many of which, particularly in the infantry divisions, were pre-war weapons. However, before the outbreak of war, new types had begun to be issued to front-line units:

- 10.5cm *leichte Feldhaubitze* (le FH – light field howitzer) 18
- 10cm *schwere Kanone* (s K – heavy cannon) 18
- 15cm *schwere Feldhaubitze* (s FH – heavy field howitzer) 18

At the end of 1942, the *Panzerhaubitz* auf *Geschützwagen* (Gw – gun carrier) I, mounting a 10.5cm *leichte Feldhaubitz* (le FH – light field howitzer) 18 on a modified PzKpfw II chassis, entered service. The type became known as the *Wespe* (wasp) and was issued to those PzDiv and PzGrenDiv equipped with the SdKfz 124 *Hummel* (bumble bee).

The 15cm sIG auf Gw 38 Ausf M *Grille* (cricket) that entered service at the beginning of 1943. The engine was installed in the centre of the chassis, allowing a larger, but open, fighting compartment to be fitted.

Initially, a gun and limber would be hauled by a team of horses, but this would change (not completely) when numbers of the powerful *schwerer Zugkraftwagen* (heavy half-track tractor) began to be issued to armoured and motorized infantry divisions. Although these vehicles were thought to have good off-road mobility, this was soon proved to be untrue by conditions encountered during the *Rasputitsa* (mud season) on the Eastern Front.

In 1940, military planners decide that a simple solution would be to position a complete 15cm s IG 33 (with gun carriage and wheels) on the chassis of a PzKpfw I Ausf B. The gun would be protected (less so the crew) by a simple, tall, box-like armoured structure that was open at the top and rear. The type was designated as the 15cm *schweres Infanteriegeschütz* (sIG) 33 *auf* PzKpfw I Ausf B. Five divisions, 1.PzDiv, 2.PzDiv, 5.PzDiv, 7.PzDiv and 9.PzDiv were each issued with a battery of six guns.

Although the chassis selected was weak and mechanically unreliable, the type showed that the concept of tracked artillery was valid and worthy of development.

In 1941, a new type of self-propelled infantry gun was produced by mounting a 15cm s IG 33 on a slightly lengthened and widened PzKpfw II chassis. A total of 12 were produced and all were issued to artillery units fighting in North Africa. But again, the chassis was mechanically unreliable, particularly with regard to engine cooling in desert conditions. No further vehicles were built and any development was cancelled.

In February 1943, the designation *Geschützwagen* (Gw – gun carrier) came into being. The first chassis chosen for conversion to carry the 15cm s IG 33 gun was that of a PzKpfw 38(t) and two types were produced: the 15cm s IG *auf* Gw 38(t) Ausf M, which had the engine at the front, and the rear-engined Ausf H. Both versions were known as the *Grille* (cricket). From 1943, every PzDiv and PzGrenDiv had a battery issued with six guns. Production of both versions ended in 1945 after some 380 had been completed.

In 1943, the artillery regiments in PzDiv and PzGrenDiv were also to be equipped with self-propelled guns. The first produced utilized a PzKpfw II chassis and entered service as the 10.5cm *leichte Feldhaubitze* 18 *auf* Gw II with the classification SdKfz 124, and were known as *Wespe* (wasp).

At the same time, a heavier armed type that utilized components from both the PzKpfw III and PzKpfw IV was about to enter service. It was classified SdKfz 165 and designated as the 15cm *schweres Feldhaubitze* 18 *auf* Gw III/IV, but was known to front-line troops as the *Hummel* (bumble bee).

Although the *Wespe* gave the field artillery unprecedented mobility, the crews had little protection from shell splinters and infantry fire. However, in reality, the PzKpfw Ii chassis had reached the end of its service life.

At the end of 1942, Alkett began producing self-propelled guns using PzKpfw II components. The type mounted a 15cm s IG 33 on a specially designed chassis, but production was halted due to a number of recurring mechanical problems.

Above: The 15cm s IG 33 was eventually mounted on the stronger and more reliable PzKpfw 38(t) chassis, providing PrGren artillery units with a self-propelled gun that could be operated over all types of terrain and adverse conditions.

Right: The chassis of the 12,000kg 15cm s IG 33 *auf* PzKpfw II was hopelessly overloaded and powered by an engine that had an inadequate cooling system for the conditions found on the North African battlefield.

Above: The 15cm s IG 33 had a maximum elevation of 75 degrees and a firing range of approximately 4,700m. In addition to firing conventional high-explosive and hollow-charge ammunition, it also could use the very effective *Stielgranate* 42, a stabilized (finned) demolition charge.

Left: Self-propelled guns such as the *Marder* II formed the backbone of the PzJg units attached to infantry divisions until the end of the war.

Battle-damaged, but drivable, tanks were frequently utilized for other duties. Here, field engineers have removed the turret from a PzKpfw 38(t) for it to be used as a supplies or ammunition carrier.

In 1942, an unknown number of artillery tractors were produced using PzKpfw 35(t) chassis. These were used to haul heavy weapons, such as the 21cm *Mörser* (mortar) 18.

Anti-aircraft Types

At the beginning of the war, German *Heeres Flugzeugabwehrkanone* (HerFlaK – army anti-aircraft gun) forces were issued with a number of different light and medium weapons:

- MG 34, sometimes in *Zwillingssockellafette* (ZwiSoLa – twin base mounting)
- 2cm FlaK 30 and 2cm FlaK 38, in single or quadruple mounting
- 3.7cm FlaK 36 and later 3.7cm FlaK 43

The units also had 8.8cm anti-aircraft guns. Up until 1943, all anti-aircraft weapons, with the exception of light guns (up to 2cm FlaK), were under the supreme command of the *Luftwaffe*.

Shortly after the outbreak of war, the light 2cm and 3.7cm anti-aircraft weapons were made mobile by mounting them on various types of half-track tractor. In this way, combat units now had some protection from attacks by ground-attack aircraft.

During the final battles in North Africa, US and British air forces had almost gained total control of the skies over the battlefield. On the Eastern Front, the Soviets also began to deploy significantly more airpower, including vast numbers of the well-armed and -armoured Ilyushin Il-2 *Shturmovik*.

In this situation, the HWa initiated the design and development of *Flakpanzer* (FlkPz – armoured anti-aircraft gun) based on tracked armoured vehicles.

In November 1943, BMM was able to present an initial solution: a 2cm FlaK 38 L/55 mounted on a Gw 38(t) Ausf M chassis fitted with a light armoured open structure to protect the weapon and crew. The type was classified as the SdKfz 140 and a total of 141 had been completed by the end of the war.

Later, half-track mounted weapons were supplemented or replaced by anti-aircraft tanks built on a simply modified PzKpfw IV chassis. The three types that entered service were the *Whirbelwind* (whirlwind), *Ostwind* (east wind) and *Möbelwagen* (furniture van).

A winter camouflaged PzKpfw 38(t) is being used to evacuate an injured soldier. The fighting compartment has been covered with metal flaps attached to the turret ring. But a lack of space inside the vehicle meant that the stretcher-borne casualty would have to be carried on the vehicle.

During the final battles in North Africa in the spring of 1943, many German tanks were lost to marauding Allied ground-attack aircraft. German military planners, under pressure due to these losses, urgently ordered the development of self-propelled armoured anti-aircraft guns. In November 1943, a small number of *Flakpanzer auf Sfl 38(t)*, each mounting a 2cm FlaK 38 L/55, entered service.

New Light Tanks 7

The first German tank developments, from the PzKpfw I to the PzKpfw IV, were the result of In6, the responsible department in the HWa, producing precise specifications. After all preparatory work had been completed, these were delivered to a manufacturer, who was then required to build prototype vehicles, frequently under demanding time constraints. All too often, experienced and combat-hardened tank crews were not involved or consulted during the design-to-prototype stage.

After a series of successful trials, a type would be accepted and ordered into production. The first tank divisions formed were issued with PzKpfw I and PzKpfw II light tanks. The PzKpfw III and PzKpfw IV then became basic equipment and served as the main battle tanks during the initial phases of the war.

In the meantime, the HWa endeavoured to develop new tank types by utilizing a combination of previous practical experience and the latest industrial technology.

In 1937, [Heinrich] Ernst Kniepkamp took over the position of *Chef-Entwickler* (chief developer) within *Waffenprüfamt* (WaPrüf – weapon testing department) 6 at the HWa. A talented engineer in civilian life, he would later be acknowledged as the designer of the HK-101, a tracked motorcycle that was built by NSU as the SdKfz 2 *Kettenkrad*.

When Kniepkamp took up his post, he immediately set down his parameters for all future tanks – firepower, armour and speed. He was also insistent that they would be built by using modern industrial technology, be armed with the most effective weaponry and be mechanically advanced. There were some at the HWa who complained that he ignored the front-line experiences of those in the *Panzertruppe* and became preoccupied with technical matters.

Kniepkamp was also responsible for encouraging Maybach-Motorenbau GmbH to design and develop a series of compact, high-performance petrol

Opposite:
The *Panzerspähwagen* (PzSpWg – armoured car) II Ausf L, known as the *Luchs* (lynx), was the most successful German-built light tank. The vehicle is in service with *Panzer-Aufklärung-Abteilung* (PzAufklAbt – armoured reconnaissance battalion) 4 attached to 4.PzDiv. Unusually, the commander wears a *Luftwaffe*-type flying helmet as used by an air liaison officer.

During the development of the PzKpfw II Ausf J, emphasis was placed on armour protection. The 80mm-thick front armour was impervious to fire from 76.2mm guns mounted in Red Army tanks. Like all PzKpfw II, the Ausf J was armed with a 2cm KwK 38 and an MG 34.

engines to power all future German tanks and specialized vehicles.

As a transmission specialist, he oversaw the design of the OLVAR hydraulically operated *Vorwählgetriebe* (pre-selector [semi-automatic] gearbox), which – although a Maybach project – was manufactured by Zahnradfabrik-Friedrichshafen (ZF) and Adlerwerke. Modern, easy-to-use technologies would also be introduced to improve steering and braking systems.

He also oversaw the introduction of torsion bar suspension carrying large diameter *Schachtellaufwerke* (interleaved [overlapping]) running wheels that allowed better driving performance. This arrangement had been in use for many years on most types of German half-track vehicles.

However, other of his proposals were rejected for various reasons – bureaucratic rivalry within the HWa, a lack of time and the precarious state of the armaments industry, which was exacerbated by the constant shortage of raw materials.

From the beginning, Kniepkamp issued the specifications for the development of a whole series of new vehicles including a surprising number of light tanks. These were classified as *Volkette* (VK – fully tracked), followed by a number to identify the weight class.

Between 1937 and 1939, not all of the projects initiated by Kniepkamp were accepted and a number never went beyond the drawing-board stage.

Above: In 1942, the prototype for an improved PzKpfw II Ausf L was designed and built with the armour on the superstructure angled in accordance with current practice. The vehicle was powered by a Tatra 103 V12-cylinder air-cooled diesel engine, as used in the *Achtrad* (8-wheeled) PzSpWg *Tropische* (TP – tropical) (SdKfz 234).

Left: In 1939, the HWa ordered the development of the PzKpfw II Ausf G to replace the PzKpfw II Ausf B, but only 45 were ever built.

When the test series of 30 PzKpfw II Ausf J were delivered at the end of 1941, its planned tactical use was no longer necessary. The tanks were then issued to special units, including the 13.*verstarkt Polizei-Panzer-Kompanie* (verst PolPzKp – re-enforced armoured police company).

Those that did were worked on by designers and engineers who had been instructed to incorporate modern technology.

As a result, contracts were issued to industry for five development vehicles, each of different combat weight, to be built. All carried the prefix VK:

- VK 601
- VK 901
- VK 1303
- VK 1601
- VK 1801

When (limited) series production began, all would be redesignated – the VK 601 and VK 1801 became PzKpfw I Ausf C and PzKpfw I Ausf F. The VK 901, VK 1303 and VK 1601, meanwhile, became the PzKpfw II Ausf G, PzKpfw II Ausf L and PzKpfw II Ausf J, respectively.

In 1942, there was no longer any need for the heavily armoured PzKpfw II Ausf F. The 30 vehicles used for trials were issued to a number of special units, such as the PzAbt 66 (zbV).

231129

The chassis of the prototype PzKpfw II Ausf J, here with a slave load to replicate the weight of a turret, was extensively trialled by the manufacturer MAN at a testing facility near their factory in Augsberg.

VK 601 – PzKpfw I Ausf C

In June 1938, the HWa issued the specification for a new type of light tank that was to be a development of the PzKpfw I. The type was given the designation VK 601 and classified as a *liechte Panzer zur Aufklärung* (light tank for reconnaissance) that was also to be used by *Fallschirmjäger* (airborne troops) units. In reality, this was a new type, since it was structurally completely different to a PzKpfw I.

While the hull and chassis developed by Krauss-Maffei were only 1.92m wide (as compared with the 2.06m width of the earlier PzKpfw I), the type nevertheless had space for a commander and a driver. The chassis was fitted with torsion bar suspension and a five-wheel, interleaved-type running gear. Initially, the rubber-pad, lubricated pin-type track, similar to that on most German half-track vehicles, was fitted. Although these allowed a speed of 80kph to be achieved on long-distance marches, wear and tear was excessive and caused many failures. Consequently, engineers at HWa decided to remedy the problem by fitting standard-type track, which – although reliable – reduced speed to 55kph.

To achieve this performance, the VK-601 was fitted with a 150hp Maybach HL 45 six -cylinder engine, driving through a ZF SSG 75 six-speed gearbox.

The superstructure and turret were designed and fabricated by Daimler-Benz.

Above: Here, *Reichsminister* Albert Speer is driving a test chassis of the PzKpfw II Ausf L *Luchs,* accompanied by Dr Ferdinand Porsche and Henschel.

Left: The PzKpfw II Ausf G was also extensively tested by Maybach-Motorenbau GmbH on a site near their factory in Friedrichshafen. The hull carries a slave weight to replicate that of the superstructure and turret.

The turret was fitted with a shallow cupola (with vision blocks), under which the commander sat between the two weapons. He was kept busy during an operation; having to direct his driver, fire and reload the weapons and also operate the radio.

The vehicle was armed with a 7.92mm MG 34, mounted on the right-hand side of the mantlet, and a Mauser 7.92mm *Einbauwaffe* (EW – built-in weapon) 141, mounted on the left.

Design of the EW 141 began in 1937 in response to a requirement for a 7.92mm MG that had a high rate of fire (100rpm) when using armour-piercing ammunition.

The HWa reported at the start of development:

> The new weapon is intended for installation in armoured vehicles, in particular the experimental reconnaissance vehicles RK 9 (*) and VK 601.

(*) The RK 9 was a wheel-cum-track vehicle.

In 1940, the EW 141, suitably modified, began to be installed as standard equipment in a number of German armoured vehicles.

The standard breech continued to be used, but the modifications meant that it could no longer be used for continuous fire. Instead, the 7.92 x 94mm *Patrone* (Ptr – cartridge) 318, as fired by the *Panzerbüchse* (PzB – anti-tank rifle) 39, was fired one at a time. The Ptr318 had a solid tungsten carbide core and a significantly larger propellant charge, giving the projectile a muzzle velocity of 1,128mps and making it possible to penetrate some 30mm of armour at 100m range and 25mm at 300m.

When the PzKpfw I Ausf C entered service in 1942, production of the EW 141, which had been long considered obsolete, came to a close.

PzKpfw I Ausf C

Year:	1942–1943
Weight:	8,000kg
Crew:	Two
Weapons:	One EW 141; one 7.92mm MG 34
Radio:	FuSprech a; later FuSprech d or f
Armour:	30mm
Engine:	150hp Maybach HL 45 six-cylinder water-cooled
Range (maximum):	300km
Speed (maximum):	80kph resp 55kph

VK 901 – PzKpfw II Ausf G

The development of this type was to run virtually in parallel to that of the VK 601, and was also specified to be fast and manoeuvrable. The vehicle was originally designated as the PzKpfw II *neuer Art* (nA – new version), armed with a 2cm KwK 30 or 2cm KwK 38 and had a combat weight of some 9,000kg.

The chassis used torsion bar suspension and five-wheeled interleaved running gear, similar to that on the PzKpfw I Ausf C. The same SSG 76 transmission was used, but the engine was replaced by a Maybach HL 62 TRM.

The hull had 30mm front armour that was considered to be safe against 2cm armour-piercing ammunition. All other surfaces were 14.5mm thick and gave protection against 7.92mm armour-piercing infantry fire. As with the PzKpfw I Ausf C, each crew member had an entry or escape hatch, a significant improvement over the early PzKpfw I and PzKpfw II.

The 2cm auto cannon installed in the turret was fitted with a vertical-stabilizing system that allowed a target to be engaged while on the move. An MG 34 was installed next to the main gun.

As a reconnaissance tank, the *Luchs* was fitted with more powerful radio equipment: a long-range *Funkgeräte* (Fu – radio device) 12, in addition to the short-range *Funksprechgeräte* (FuSprGer – two-way radio [transceiver]) f, which had a range of up to 70km when attached to a d.

The initial order for a 0 series of 75 vehicles was not completed, and only 45 were delivered as the PzKpfw II Ausf G. Plans were being made, even while the type was still undergoing trials, for the production of an initial 500 followed by another 250. However, the project was cancelled, as were any further developments, including a version armed with a conical-barrelled 2.8cm KwK.

In 1941, the HWa issued the specification for a self-propelled tank destroyer based on the chassis of the VK 901. The weapon selected was a specially modified 5cm PaK 38, protected by an open-topped armoured shield.

Again, military planners, possibly being pressurized by the situation on the Eastern Front, decided that 1,200 of the type would be required for the tank destroyer elements in infantry divisions, and a further 800 would be issued to the tank destroyer and reconnaissance elements in each PzDiv.

Although series production never happened, the two prototypes of the *Panzer-Selbstfahrlafette* (PzSfl – armoured self-propelled) I c built were issued to PzJgAbt 559 in March 1942 and used on the Eastern Front.

PzKpfw II Ausf G

Year:	1942–1943
Weight:	10,500kg
Crew:	Three
Weapons:	One 2cm KwK 38; one 7.92mm MG 34
Radio:	FuSprech a; later FuSprech d or f
Armour:	30mm
Engine:	140hp Maybach HL 62 TRM six-cylinder, water-cooled
Speed (maximum):	65kph

A *Luchs* was fitted with four exit or escape hatches, one for each of the four crewmen. It also had *Schachtellaufwereke* (interleaved [overlapping] running wheels) that allowed the vehicle to achieve a top speed of 60kph.

VK 1303 – PzKpfw II Ausf L

In September 1939, the HWa initiated the development of a fully tracked armoured vehicle that was to be specifically issued to the *Panzeraufklärungs-Abteilungen* (PzAufklAbt – armoured reconnaissance battalions). In terms of off-road mobility, the superiority of tracked vehicles over the wheeled armoured cars was obvious. The new vehicle was very similar to the VK 901, but was designed to have space for a fourth crew member.

The shape of the hull was basically identical in design, but slightly larger. The vehicle was powered by a Maybach HL 66 P, that drove a conventional ZF Synchron SSG 46 six-speed manually operated gearbox.

The turret was slightly larger, so as to accommodate a gunner, and an additional hatch was fitted in the rear wall, as on the PzKpfw I Ausf C.

The enlarged hull allowed a FuSpech f transceiver and a long-range Fu 12 to be installed in vehicles issued to a company commander and battalion staff. In addition to the *Stabsantenne* mounted on the turret, the vehicles had an additional star-type aeriel d mounted on the right-hand side of the superstructure.

The barrel of the 2cm KwK 38 cannon was 300mm longer than the earlier 2cm KwK 30.

The initial plan was to produce the VK 901 and VK 1303 in identical quantities of 250 vehicles each. In March 1942, production VK 901 was halted and priority given to the VK 1303, which was probably a logical decision. When the type entered service, it was designated PzKpfw II Ausf L and became known as the *Luchs* (lynx), but all production of the type ceased after a total of 100 had been completed.

Interestingly, military planners had, even before production began, decided to install a 5cm KwK L/60 as the main armament after 100 VK 1303 had

PzKpfw II Ausf L *Luchs*

Year:	1942–1943
Weight:	11,800kg
Crew:	Four
Weapons:	One 2cm KwK 38; one 7.92mm MG 34
Radio:	FuSprech f transceiver; Fu 12 radio
Armour:	30mm
Engine:	180hp Maybach HL 66 P six-cylinder, water-cooled
Range (maximum):	260km
Speed (maximum):	60kph

been delivered to front-line units. The decision, as recorded in an original HWa specification sheet, is quite understandable considering that the 2cm KwK could not defeat the armour on the latest enemy tanks.

VK 1801 – PzKpfw I Ausf F

In the 1930s, the OKH developed a new doctrine for ground forces of the *Wehrmacht* by perfecting the *Blitzkrieg* (lightning) attack executed by highly mobile tank units.

At the same time, military planners recognized that bordering countries had begun building a number of well-armed defensive fortifications. Consequently, German forces demanded the urgent development of heavily armoured tanks capable of defeating guns emplaced in the walls and adjacent bunkers, and also of providing support fire for attacks by assault pioneers and infantry.

However, the defensive border fortress that inspired these plans had already become obsolete before the war began.

Czechoslovakia had erected what was considered to be a modern bunker system and hoped German commanders would see it as a serious obstacle. However, few fortifications encountered in Poland were easily by-passed, proving to be of little use to the defenders.

Fortresses such as Ében-Émael in Belgium and the Maginot Line in France were of a different quality. But even these well-designed and expensively built structures were successfully neutralized during the advance on France, despite having armoured gun emplacements.

In winter, snow and slush was a constant problem for the crews of all tracked vehicles. Here a crewman uses a pickaxe to clear the track links on a PzKpfw II Ausf F.

Although German forces had found the Czechoslovak and Polish fortresses to be ineffective, the HWa issued the specification for an 18,000kg-class tank (designed to avoid exceeding the load capacity when carrying bridging equipment) in December 1939. But for an unknown reason, the HWa did not cancel the project, even though the original purpose for such a vehicle had proven to be outdated.

As late as July 1942, the project was still being described as a 'further development of the PzKpfw I with a focus on the heaviest armour'. As a result, the turret and superstructure were fabricated from 80mm plate, with 60mm for the rear of the hull. The type was armed with two 7.92mm MG 34 mounted in the turret and operated by the commander.

Initially, the production of the first series of 100 vehicles was authorized, but this was later reduced to 30 before the order was cancelled.

In July 1942, the VK 1801 entered service as the PzKpfw I Ausf F and all of the 30 produced were delivered between April and December 1942.

PzKpfw I Ausf F	
Year:	1941–1942
Weight:	21,000kg
Crew:	Three
Weapons:	One 2cm KwK 38; two 7.92mm MG 34
Radio:	FuSprech a, d or f transceiver
Armour:	80mm
Engine:	150hp Maybach HL 45 P, six-cylinder, water-cooled
Range (maximum:	150km
Speed (maximum):	25kph

VK 1601 – PzKpfw II Ausf J

In 1939, the HWa initiated the development of a PzKpfw II nA *verstärkt* (verst – reinforced armour). Although the vehicle was intended for combat reconnaissance, it was to have armour that could withstand fire from enemy 75mm weapons.

Production of an initial series of 30 vehicles was planned, but after the successful completion of intensive trials, the HWa placed an order for 700 of the type.

All were issued to PzDiv for battlefield reconnaissance and also to the artillery as PzBeobWg.

The 18,000kg-class vehicle was very similar to the VK 1801 and had interleaved running gear and wide tracks.

The type was armed with a 2cm KwK 38 and a 7.92mm MG 34 mounted in a small turret that only had space for the commander, who was also the gunner and loader.

PzKpfw II Ausf J

Year:	1941–1942
Weight:	18,000kg
Crew:	Three
Weapons:	One 2cm KwK 38; one 7.92mm MG 34
Radio:	FuSprech d or f
Armour:	Front 80mm; sides and rear 50mm
Engine:	150hp Maybach HL 45 six-cylinder, water-cooled
Range (maximum):	150km
Speed (maximum):	25kph

In September 1943, the 13.verst PolKp was deployed in Yugoslavia with six PzSpWg, five PzKpfw II Ausf J and five PzKpfw IV Ausf F (7.5cm KwK L/24).

Development work on all new light tanks was significantly cut back in 1942, possibly as an attempt to improve the disastrously poor level of tank production. In December 1941, Hitler once again interfered with development work being carried out by In 6:

> The Führer considers it necessary, given our extremely strained and limited manufacturing capabilities, including the lack of skilled workers, raw materials and production capacity, to limit the tank programme in terms of the different types and to determine the future types. The Führer calls for a simplification and limitation in order to facilitate mass production (standardization of engines, gearboxes, running gear and tracks). The Führer has the following five basic types in mind:
>
> • Fast (reconnaissance) tank
> • Medium tank (based on previous PzKpfw IV)
> • Heavy tank (Porsche, Henschel)

- Super heavy tank
- Infantry assault gun (Based on PzKpfw IV)

The Führer [*] wishes to make this decision personally and to speak to *Oberst* Fichtner [**] about this and also to Dr Porsche [***] after his forthcoming trip to the front. The commander-in-chief of the army is free to take part in the meeting.

[*] Hitler, whose simplification of the tank programme was typical of his erratic interference in technical matters.

[**] *Oberst* Sebastian Fichtner worked as an engineer in the HWa from 1933 to 1942 and was significantly involved in the development of the PzKpfw VI Ausf E Tiger. In 1942, he became the commander of 8.PzDiv.

[***] Dr Ferdinand Porsche was to become more significantly involved in German tank development and production as head of the newly established tank commission in late 1941.

Although the PzKpfw II Ausf F was a small tank, it weighed 21,000kg, almost the same as the larger PzKpfw IV.

PzKpfw 38(t) nA

In parallel with the work on the VK projects, BMM, the manufacturer of the PzKpfw 38(t), was to begin work on the PzKpfw 38(t) nA. Their aim was to redesign the original tank as a reconnaissance vehicle, despite it being seen as an alternative to the VK 901 and VK 1303.

The new tank was almost identical to the PzKpfw 38(t). The superstructure on the first test vehicle was riveted as before, but this was changed in favour of welding for all production vehicles.

In order to achieve the required high speed of some 53kph, the designers decided to install a 220hp Praga V8 petrol engine. The well-proven Škoda

The PzKpfw 38(t) *Neue art* (nA – new version) was purposely designed as a reconnaissance tank and fitted with a turret that had improved observation devices. The vehicle is being examined by Adolf Hitler and Albert Speer. The civilian is Dr Ferdinand Porsche, who attended many of these events whether he was involved with a project or not.

PzKpfw 38(t) nA

Year: 1942
Weight: 10,600kg
Crew: Four
Weapons: One 3.7cm KwK 38 L/48; one 7.92mm MG 34
Radio: FuSprech d or f
Armour: Front 50mm; sides and rear 30mm
Engine: 220hp Praga EPA, V8-cylinder, water-cooled
Range   (maximum): 200km
Speed   (maximum): 52.5kph

3.7cm tank gun and a 7.92mm MG 34 were installed in the turret. There had originally been a plan to fit a larger turret, mounting a 5cm KwK 39/1, but this was not pursued further.

Interestingly, the project was listed as a PzSpWg Ausf II BMM. But, even after the type had been thoroughly and successfully tested, the HWa decided to halt development.

An additional number of reconnaissance tanks were produced by modifying a standard PzKpfw 38(t).

In Action

At the beginning of the design and development process, the VK 601, VK 901, VK 1303, VK 1601 and VK 1801 were all intended to enter production, and

Thanks to its robust construction, strong armour and massive tracks, the PzKpfw II Ausf J could survive the detonation of simple anti-tank mines without damage.

sometimes in large numbers, even by German standards. But because of the lengthy development processes, many of their basic mission requirements were already outdated by the time they were ready for production. Consequently, the orders were revised and all types, with one exception, were manufactured as a limited 0 series. The exception was the PzKpfw II Ausf L, and of 100 vehicles produced, approximately 30 were issued to each of two units in the PzAufklAbt attached to 4.PzDiv and 9.PzDiv. The remainder were held in reserve as replacement vehicles. The light reconnaissance tanks were used successfully for the first time during the German offensive on the Kursk Salient.

Of the previously mentioned VK vehicles, 40 VK 601, 30 VK 1801, 45 VK 901 and 30 VK 1601 were not scrapped but issued to various, often small, units for special tasks.

Malta

The island was to play a major strategic role as the North Africa campaign evolved. The Royal Navy (RN) had port and dockyard facilities in Valletta and the Royal Air Force (RAF) flew from three airfields – Luqa, Hal Far and Ta Qali – allowing both services to launch virtually unchallenged attacks on German aircraft and shipping tasked with transporting supplies to North Africa.

But in December 1941, the situation changed when Hitler ordered the formation of *Luftflotte* (air fleet) 2, commanded by *Generalfeldmarschall* Albert Kesselring, and deployed it to airfields on Sicily. From there, assisted by units of the Italian Air Force, the *Luftwaffe* began round-the-clock bombing of British airfields and naval facilities on Malta. As a result, British operations against German supply routes came to a virtual halt.

Interestingly, German high command in the Mediterranean had, since the end of 1940, been preparing a plan, code-named *Unternehmen Herkules* (Operation Hercules), for an amphibious landing to capture Malta. However, it was postponed several times, partly because, after his successful summer offensive against the British Eighth Army, Rommel had assured Hitler that he would be able to reach the Nile despite the threat to his supply lines.

This was ultimately negligent. *Luftflotte* 2 had been withdrawn, allowing supplies to reach the island and replacement aircraft to be delivered to the RAF squadrons on Malta. Subsequently, the attacks on Axis shipping resumed and severely disrupted those supplies destined for German and Italian units in North Africa. Once again, a lack of supplies weakened their ability to fight – this time decisively.

From August to October 1942, some 30 percent of all transports were sunk or shot down. In October 1942 alone, four tankers carrying 60 percent of the fuel required were sunk by British forces. The plan for *Herkules* was simple.

British ground forces were considered to be quite manageable having only 10 tanks to support operations. The only problem that concerned the potential invaders were the four Infantry Tank Mk II Matilda.

In order to have clear superiority during the critical landing phase, special unit PzAbt 66 (zbV), partly issued with heavily armoured tanks that had been captured from the Red Army, was deployed. The KV-1 and KV-2 were issued to 2.Kp, which was the lead company of the first wave and ordered to break the toughest resistance. Meanwhile, 1.Kp was issued with five PzKpfw I Ausf F, five PzKpfw II Ausf J and 12 PzKpfw IV Ausf G armed with a 7.5cm KwK 40 L/43.

Combat in the East

Although the planned invasion of Malta was finally cancelled in 1943, it had already been decided, in the summer of 1942, to transfer the PzAbt 66 (zbV) to the Soviet battlefront. The ultimate destination of the KV-1 and KV-2 captured tanks cannot be determined, although it can be presumed that 2.Kp/ PzAbt (zbV) 66 was disbanded and their tanks issued to other units.

Like the PzKpfw II Ausf J, the PzKpfw II Ausf F was originally developed to attack fortifications and bunkers. Although this was no longer an essential requirement after two years of war, work on both types continued.

The 1.Kp/PzAbt (zbV) 66 was transferred to PzRgt 29 (12.PzDiv) that was fighting, as part of HG *Nord*, near the city of Leningrad. The well-armoured vehicles were used there to combat heavily fortified enemy positions – the purpose for which the vehicles were created. During the course of the operation, the unit was renamed 8.Kp/PzRgt 29.

Similar to the PzKpfw VI Ausf E Tiger of s PzAbt 502, which were used there, albeit in small numbers, for the first time, the PzKpfw I Ausf F and

PzKpfw II Ausf J were severely limited in use due to their considerable weight. The constantly swampy ground in the forests of northern Russia forced the construction of a system of dry areas, created by building simple dams from branches and tree trunks. When missions were ordered, the tanks would be driven onto the dry area to provide fire support for the infantry. Breakthroughs were not possible because any movement away from the prepared area was impossible, despite both types being virtually immune to anti-tank mines.

Elements of PzAufklAbt 9 loaded on railway wagons, ready to be transported to the battlefront. Initially, it was planned to arm a variant of the *Luchs* with a 5cm KwK 39, but this project, like many others initiated by the HWa, was cancelled.

In 1939, the half-track manufacturer, Krausse-Maffei, produced a prototype for a new type of light tank intended as a replacement for the PzKpfw I. The type was designated PzKpfw I Ausf C, armed with a 7.62mm Ew 141 and built using the latest technology available to German industry. A total of 40 were completed, but none entered front-line service, instead being issued to tank training establishments.

Anti-partisan Operations

In July 1942, *SS-Polizei Regiment* (PolRgt – police regiment) 14 was established in southern Russia to prevent local partisan units from carrying out sabotage and other actions. At the beginning of 1943, SS-PolRgt 14 was sent to Marseille, France, for rest and replenishment and was assigned a 13.Kp, equipped with six VK 1601 and a number of armoured personnel carriers. The regiment remained there until July 1943, when it was attached to the *Oberbefehlshaber Südost* (commander-in-chief Southeast) and deployed for security tasks in occupied Yugoslavia. Under the command of III.SS-Panzer Corps, anti-partisan operations were carried out near Delnice, and on the railway network around Novo Mesto in Slovenia.

Despite being relatively heavy, the VK 1601 performed surprisingly well in the rock-strewn mountain environment, and mechanical repairs were usually quickly completed.

What was probably the last VK 1601 deployment took place at the end of 1944, near the city of Memel in East Prussia. In autumn 1944, *Panzer-Sicherungs-Kompanie* (PzSichKp – armoured security company) 350 was established in the field and issued with 10 PzKpfw II Ausf J.

During the course of 1943, those PzKpfw II Ausf J in service with 13.verst PolPzKp were repainted to suit the conditions in Yugoslavia. The original *dunkel grau* (dark grey) was changed to a *dunkel gelb* (dark yellow) with a *grün streifen* (green stripe) camouflage scheme.

Reconnaissance

The 40 VK 601 built were, for an unknown reason, initially kept in reserve. At the beginning of 1943, two of the type and eight VK 1801 were issued to PzRgt 1 for deployment in the Soviet Union. In September 1943, the remaining 38 VK 601 were issued to LVIII.Panzer Corps in France, where they were to be used to train tank crews. At least one of these vehicles was assigned to s PzAbt 503 when it was being reorganized in France.

Projects and the Enemy 8

After the delivery of the last PzKpfw II Ausf F in July 1942, large-scale production of light tanks in Germany ended. At about the same time, the last of the more modern light tank designs from the VK series rolled off the assembly line. Some of these types were originally intended to be produced in large quantities. However, those decisions were all reversed.

The reason for this has largely to do with the limited capacities of German industry and its poor raw material supplies. The war demanded that all available resources be used to produce the required number of battle tanks. For the same reasons, the planned conversion of the production of the PzKpfw IV to the PzKpfw V Panther could never be carried out.

The July 1942, *Rüststandsmeldungen* (armament status report), compiled monthly by the HWa, stated that there were still some 700 PzKpfw I (including VK 1801) in service. There were also 1,000 vehicles from all construction lots of the PzKpfw II (2cm KwK) available, including the VK 901 and VK 1601. These summary figures included all vehicles in the field army and the reserve army. A separate list was only to be introduced for the VK 1303, presumably because there was still an extensive production order at that time; there were plans to build almost 2,000 of these reconnaissance tanks by April.

The PzKpfw I were only used for secondary tasks and in the replacement establishments as training vehicles. Apparently, the old chassis soon wore out and were scrapped.

The PzKpfw II were used extensively in the light platoons of the tank companies and the staff companies of the tank regiments and battalions, which had five vehicles each. At the beginning of the major summer offensive in July 1942, HG *Süd* (south),which had 19 armoured and eight motorized units, still had around 400 of these combat vehicles in its inventory. By the time of *Unternehmen Zitadelle* (Operation Citadel), almost a year later, the number

Opposite: In 1939, the Red Army had some 7,500 battle-ready BT-5 and BT-7 light tanks in service. Both mounted a 45mm M1932 main gun that could defeat all types of light tank in service with the *Panzerwaffe.*

of PzKpfw II had fallen to 100. The remaining units were distributed across the Eastern Front. The *Panzerarmee Afrika* probably also had similarly small numbers.

The PzKpfw II were used for battlefield reconnaissance and security tasks, and were also used for a variety of other purposes, such as *Kommandowagen* (command vehicle), *Munitionswagen* (ammunition vehicle) and supply carriers.

From August 1942, available chassis of the PzKpfw II, as well as the PzKpfw 38(t), were preferably used for the production of self-propelled guns (7.5cm PaK 40 on the PzKpfw II, *Marder* II). This also included the majority of tanks that were badly damaged in action and were delivered to Germany for general repairs.

At the end of 1942, production of the 10.5cm *Panzerhaubitze auf* Gw II *Wespe* self-propelled howitzer commenced. The components used for the Gw II were adopted practically unchanged from the PzKpfw II. The total number was 676 vehicles.

Many PzKpfw II were lost in combat operations throughout 1943, but a total of 400 vehicles remained listed in the *Rüststandsmeldungen*, dated February 1944. This number was supposed to increase to 446 by July 1944, probably through repairs. The following month, the PzKpfw II was to be removed from the armament status reports for reasons now unknown.

After Germany ceased the production of light tanks, the *Jagdpanzer* (JgdPz – hunting tank) 38, known as the *Hetzer*, was assembled using a number of components from the PzKpfw 38(t). By the end of the war, more than 2,500 vehicles had been built.

In 1944, Auto-Union was contracted to design and develop a tracked armoured personnel carrier with capacity for eight fully equipped PzGren. The vehicle was fitted with torsion bar suspension and, in accordance with current German design practice, *Schachtellaufwerke* (overlapping [interleaved] road wheels). The project was called *Kätzchen* (kitten).

Some important tasks of the light tanks in the tank divisions, such as tactical reconnaissance, were now carried out by those platoons in le PzDiv equipped with PzKpfw IV and PzKpfw V Panther.

E-Series Project

The HWa, although completely aware of the perilous state of the German heavy and armaments industry, continued to draft specifications and issue contracts to various companies for the design and development of future armoured vehicles.

In 1941, Kniepkamp was appointed *Oberbaurat* (senior construction officer) of a newly established department in the HWa, that soon became known as his '*Forschungsgruppe*' (research group).

One of their first projects was the development of sloping armour that, after ballistic testing, was used for the first time when production of the PzKpfw V Panther began in 1942.

After this first success, Kniepkamp and his team began to concentrate their effort on the development of a completely new generation of German tanks. This resulted in the *Entwicklungstypen-Serie* (E – type development series), which broke with convention by initiating programmes for the design of entire series of tanks, rather than commissioning a specific type for design and development.

- E-10 – Light tank destroyer
- E-25 – Medium tank destroyer
- E-50 – Medium tank (to replace the PzKpfw V Panther)

The second test vehicle for the *Kätzchen* (kitten) was delivered by BMM at the end of 1944. It was fitted with much simpler leaf-spring suspension and utilized a number of components from the JgdPz 38.

- E-75 – Heavy tank (to replace the PzKpfw VI Ausf B Tiger II)
- E-100 – Super-heavy tank

Due to the lack of production capacity in the armaments industry, the HWa was forced to place the contracts for the design, development and manufacture of the new series with five companies that had little or no previous experience of building tanks – Adlerwerke in Frankfurt-am-Main, Argus-Motoren in Karlsruhe, Eisenwerke Weserhütte in Bad Oeynhausen and Klöckner Humboldt Deutz (KHD) in Ulm. However, Adlerwerke did have experience in building half-track vehicles.

Kniepkamp, at the beginning, used his authority to ensure that his team had access to the very latest technology, but the situation in Germany eventually forced him to relent and use whatever was available.

In order to keep the vehicle compact and within the specified weight limits, the design team was forced to make a number of bold changes. They decided not use the well-proven torsion bar suspension, but instead fitted externally mounted vertical conical springs while retaining interleaved running wheels. On both the E-10 and E-25, the designers decided to position the engine, transmission and steering system in a bay in the rear section of the hull to make a much more spacious fighting compartment. The superstructure, that had sloping front, side and rear surfaces, was fabricated from the most effective armour available.

Finally, the specification required most components on the E-10 and E-25, particularly the engine, transmission, suspension, running gear and tracks, to be interchangeable. The same also applied to the E-50, E-75 and, to a limited extent, E-100. Although the E-10 and E-25 were initially designed as tank destroyers, both could have easily been used as a light tank.

However, due to the dire economic situation and grave state of German industry, the planned E-series of advanced tanks would never be realized. Only a test hull was built for the super-heavy E-100.

Panzer 38D

It must have become obvious to Kniepkamp and his team that, due to the continuing decline in German industrial output, their ambitious plans for the E-series would never come to fruition. In 1944, as an alternative, they began the process of evaluating as to whether the hull and mechanical components of the *Jagdpanzer* (JgdPz – tank hunter) 38 could be utilized to produce a new series of armoured vehicles.

BMM planned a complete series of combat and support vehicles based on the PzKpfw 38 D. This design of a reconnaissance tank was to be armed with the 2cm KwK 38 in a *Hängelafette* (hanging mount). (Hilary L. Doyle)

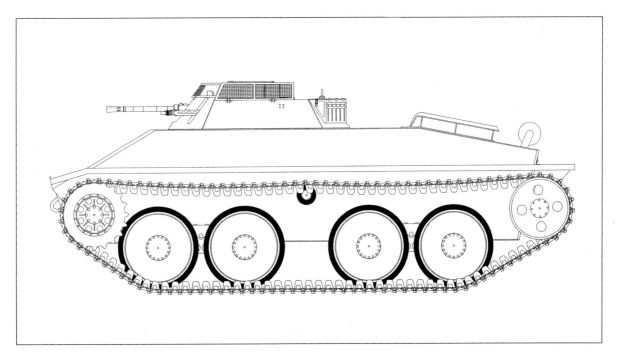

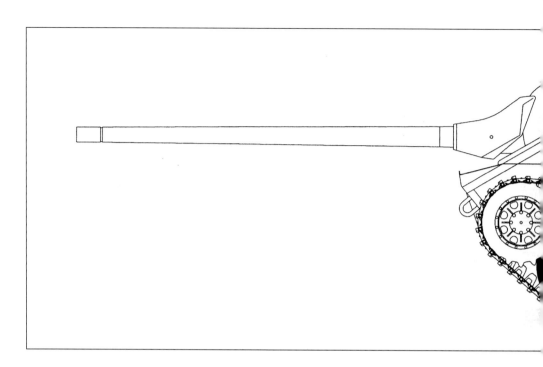

Subsequently, the HWa issued orders for two types to be developed with some urgency, but due to a lack of time, both would be armed with a readily available weapon. It was proposed that one version should be fitted with the same type of open-topped turret as used on a SdKfz 250/9 *Panzerspähwagen* (PzSpWg – armoured reconnaissance car). The other version was built as a self-propelled carriage mounting a 7.5cm K 51 L/24 fitted with a three-sided open shield.

As the requirement for mobile artillery grew more desperate, the HWa issued the specifications for a series of self-propelled guns carried on the simple, but reliable, Panzer 38 D chassis. This would be achieved by lengthening the hull and running gear, utilizing many of the existing mechanical components

Panzer 38 D (proposed)

Year:	Never built
Weight:	18,000kg
Crew:	Four
Armament:	One 7.5cm KwK 40 L/48; one 7.92mm MG 42
Armour:	60mm
Engine:	210hp Tatra 103 V12-cylinder, air-cooled, diesel,
Range (maximum):	500km
Speed (maximum):	45kph

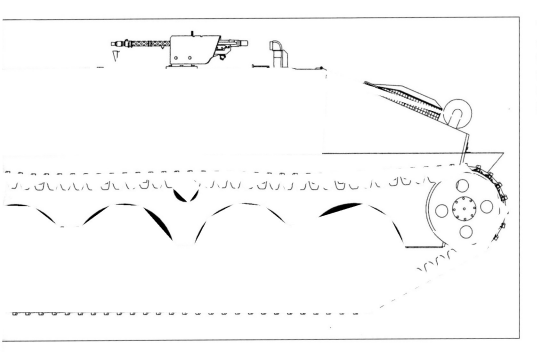

The Jagdpanzer 38 D was designed to carry the 7.5cm KwK 42 L/70 tank gun, as mounted in the PzKpfw V Panther. (Hilary L. Doyle)

and fitting the newly developed 14,825cc Tatra V12-cylinder, air-cooled diesel engine.

Originally, the HWa planned for three versions to be produced – a tank destroyer mounting a 7.5cm StuK 42 L/70; a light tank mounting a 7.5cm KwK 40 L/48 in a rotatable turret, and a reconnaissance tank mounting a 2cm KwK L/38 or 7.5cm KwK 51 L/24.

Finally, in response to a requirement issued by the *Panzerartillerie* (armoured artillery) in 1944, the chassis was utilized for a *Waffenträger groß* (large weapon carrier) I carrying a 10.5cm le FH 18/40 L/28. The chassis was then lengthened again for a *Waffenträger groß* II that mounted either a 12.8cm PaK 44 L/55, 15cm s FH 18 L/29.5 or 8.8cm PaK 43 L/71.

All the above projects, like the E-series models, were still at the design or development stage when the war in Europe ended on 5 May 1945.

Allied Light Tanks

Before World War II, Britain, France, the Soviet Union and other nations all equipped and organized their armoured forces in a similar way. However, Germany, under guidance from Keinz Guderian, took a totally different path.

The victorious powers of World War I were free to advance their respective rearmament programmes, whereas Germany was shackled by the conditions set out in the Treaty of Versailles. The winning states were, however, subject constraints of other kinds.

Great Britain was in recession and its economic problems left it unable to find the funding required for a consistent rearmament programme. Also, a large part of the population had become anti-military after the privations they had faced during the years of World War I.

On 6 April 1917, the US government declared war on the German Empire and sent forces to France. After the war, the country remained economically strong but the government, under pressure from its population, was forced to adopt a series of neutrality laws to prevent US involvement in any future conflicts.

Great Britain

Britain had an efficient armaments industry that supplied the British Army and many other nations around the world. In the 1930s, a clear three-part division for equipment of the British armoured force emerged. Small or light tanks were used for battlefield reconnaissance. Cruiser tanks were intended to achieve the operational breakthrough of enemy lines. Heavily armoured and slow-moving infantry tanks were placed directly under the command of the infantry.

Carden-Loyd was a leader in the development and production of light tanks until it was taken over by Vickers in 1938. The first tankettes gave rise to a series of light tanks built using simple and cost-effective technology. The hull and superstructure were fabricated from steel plates riveted to internal frames,

The British-built Medium Mk II being recovered on a trailer attached to a pre-production Scammel Pioneer heavy road tractor. Note the rear driving wheels are fitted with cleated bands to improve traction. (Getty)

The Vickers Medium Mk I and Mk II mounted a OQF 3-Pounder gun. Another version, the Medium Mk IIA CS, mounted a 3.7in howitzer to provide supporting fire for the infantry.

and the movable roller carriage-type running gear was suspended on external coil springs.

The engine, transmission and drive were housed at the front. A rotatable turret attached to the rear of the superstructure carried the machine-gun armament. The Light Tank Mk II, Mk III and Mk IV each mounted a 0.303in Vickers MG, but the Mk V carried an additional 0.50in Vickers heavy MG. The most important, in terms of numbers built, was the final variant, the Mk VI, some of which mounted a 15mm Besa MG as the main armament (Mk VIC).

Light Tank Mk VIC

After deliveries of the Mk VIC had been completed, the directors of Vickers Carden-Loyd decided that the company would stop building small combat vehicles. Although the light tank had proven to be of value in the colonies, those in France were found to be seriously inferior to the light tanks of the *Panzerwaffe*.

In 1937, the same directors had a change of mind and commissioned the development of a larger version. The Light Tank Mk VI had a different drive system with four wheels of the same size. The noticeably larger turret carried a OQF 2-Pdr gun. Alternatively, the Mk VI CS was armed with a 3in howitzer – a significant increase in firepower.

The Lease-Lease Program, signed on 11 March 1941, meant that Great Britain began to receive the US-built Light Tank M3 (Stuart Mk I–Mk V), and as the supply increased, some 170 were delivered to British tank forces fighting in the deserts of North Africa. The type was reliable, fast, manoeuvrable and gave crews a smooth ride over the desert terrain, for which they named it the 'Honey'. The type was armed with a 37mm Gun M5 or Gun M6, which could defeat all German – and Italian – tanks before better-armoured and -armed medium tanks arrived in mid-1942.

As the war progressed, the British Army changed its requirements and the light tank was replaced by an increasing number of armoured cars.

The Light Tank Mk VI was the standard reconnaissance tank of the British forces until 1942. It used a Carden-Loyd chassis without an idler wheel. The engine and transmission were fitted at the front. The Mk VIB was armed with 7.7mm and 12.7mm machine guns in the turret.

France

At the beginning of World War II, France had a bewildering number of different light tank types in service, including a significant amount of Renault FT, even though the type had long been considered obsolete.

Other types, the Forges Chantiers de la Méditerranée (FCM) 36, Renault R-35 and R-40, and Hotchkiss H-35, H-38 and H-39, were primarily used to support the infantry.

From 1933, the French army began to receive the more modern *Automitrailleuse de Reconnaissance* (AMR – armoured reconnaissance vehicle) 33 and AMR 35, which were also assigned to the motorized infantry as support vehicles. Both types were very fast for the time and were therefore well suited for reconnaissance purposes, but suffered from major mechanical problems.

For Renault, the manufacturer responsible for development and production, the type was a financial disaster. In all vehicles, parts of the transmission had to be replaced several times at the company's expense.

Since this fiasco was foreseeable early on, the French concentrated on wheeled armoured vehicles such, as the successful Panhard P178 *Automitrailleuse de Découverte* (AMD – armoured observation vehicle).

The Renault *Automitrailleuse de Reconnaissance* (AMR) 33 light cavalry tank, was to be mass-produced for the French Army but, in fact, only some 100 vehicles were procured. Many of these were deployed to support motorized infantry during the invasion of France. The two-man tank was mechanically unreliable, poorly armed and inadequately armoured.

Above: The French decided to use wheeled armoured cars, rather than tanks, for combat reconnaissance. The Panhard P178 was a well-balanced, powerful and advanced vehicle that was appreciated by the *Wehrmacht*, who continued to use captured vehicles until 1945.

Left: In 1936, the Renault *Automitrailleuse de Combat* (AMC – armoured combat vehicle) 35 was designed as a cavalry tank and armed with a powerful 47mm SA 35 anti-tank gun.

Soviet Union

The Soviet Union began the mass introduction of tanks long before World War II. However, due to a lack of technical expertise, production licences were acquired from various foreign manufacturers, whose existing designs were then adapted so that the vehicles would be better suited to the country's terrain and weather conditions.

The first licence to be acquired was for the Renault FT. The type was designated MS-1 or T-18 by the Red Army and approximately 1,000 were eventually

The Soviet-built T-26 was designed as an infantry tank, whereas the BT-5 and BT-7 were both designed as fast cavalry tanks. Despite being very different, all three mounted the same armament and had limited armour protection.

built in the Soviet Union. Due to its size and weight, it was a true light tank but, like the original, it did not meet with modern battlefield requirements. In 1930, a number of licences were acquired from the British company Vickers-Armstrongs Limited. Soviet engineers used the Carden-Loyd Tankette as the basis for the T-27. The two-man vehicle was found to be too small and the Red Army could not find sufficient men of short stature to crew the type. By 1934, over 3,000 T-27 had been manufactured, but they were considered obsolete and of little combat value by the beginning of World War II.

German soldiers on a T-26 abandoned by the Red Army. The type was truly obsolete when German forces launched *Unternehmen Barbarossa* on 22 June 1941. It is thought that some 10,000 had been built before World War II.

T-26

Among the vehicles for which the soviets acquired a licence was the Vickers 6-ton tank. The type had relatively thin 19mm–25mm armour, but was powered by a 98hp Armstrong Siddeley petrol engine (also built under licence) that gave the 7,000kg vehicle acceptable speed and mobility.

The Soviet designation for the type was T-26 M 1931 when it was fitted with two MG turrets, and T-26 M 1933 when it was fitted with a large turret mounting a Soviet-designed 45mm 20K gun.

As production of the T-26 continued, its design progressively developed. As early as 1935, a welded turret with slightly sloping sides was introduced on the M 1935. The M 1939 was the final version, and featured a hull with sloping sides to improve amour protection.

More than 10,000 of the type were produced, making it the most widely used tank of its era. The T-26 first saw action during the Spanish Civil War and during the Battle of Lake Khasan, also known as the Changkufeng Incident (29 July– 11 August 1938). In both actions, the tank proved to be effective, although this success is somewhat tempered by the relative weakness of its opponent.

BT Series

The BT series was developed in parallel with the T-26. These fast (cavalry) tanks were based on the designs of the US engineer J. Walter Christie. He had been offering his groundbreaking tanks to the US Army for years without success. But Russian diplomats working in the US were closely observing his work and began sending reports to military planners in the Soviet Union.

Christie designed his armoured vehicles as hybrid types, in which the compact running gear of four large-diameter wheels could be operated with tracks in order to achieve maximum off-road mobility. Alternatively, the tracks could be removed and stowed on the tank, allowing high-speed travel over paved roads. The vehicle was driven from the rear sprocket via a Gall chain to the two rear running wheels. Christie tanks were powered by a 400hp Liberty L-12 petrol engine and capable of remarkably high speeds (for a tank) in both driving modes.

In 1931, Russian agents were able to procure two turretless Christie tanks and export both, falsely documented as agricultural tractors, to the Soviet Union. The first Russian version was the *Bystrokhodnyy tank* (BT – fast tank) 2, which entered production in 1932. The BT-5 that entered service in 1933 was the most produced version and was fitted with a T-26 turret mounting a 45mm 20K gun. In 1935, this was followed by the BT-7 fitted with a T-26 M 1935 turret mounting a 76.2mm KT-26 howitzer, which was very effective against soft targets. Like the BT-5, the BT-7 was also built in large numbers (more than 7,500 in total).

Inventor J. Walter Christie designed the M1928 (later the M1931) track-cum-wheel tank for the US Cavalry. After trials, the prototypes were returned to Christie, where they were spotted by Soviet agents. Both were purchased and secretly sent to Russia, where they were used to develop the *Bystrokhodnyy* Tank (BT – high-speed tank). The first production vehicle was designated BT-2 and armed with the 37mm M30 gun. (Getty)

Light Amphibious Tanks

Western Russia has a very demanding terrain and a climate that has strong seasonal fluctuations. Heavy storms often occur in late summer and autumn, bringing rain that, due to the type of soil, cannot easily drain off the land. This results in vast areas flooding, turning the land into fields of deep, impassible mud that severely limit the passage of motor vehicles, especially heavy armoured types.

In the 1930s, the transport infrastructure in the Soviet Union was poorly developed, being limited to railway lines and a few hard-surfaced main roads. It is not surprising, then, that the development of the light tank in Russia has

Amphibious light tanks entered Red Army service before the outbreak of World War II. The T-38, like the earlier T-37, carried a two-man crew and was armed with a 7.62mm Degtyarev DT machine gun. The vehicle was primarily used for reconnaissance duties. (Getty)

T-37A and T-38

British-designed types were once again used. The buoyant Vickers-Carden-Loyd light amphibious tank developed in 1930/31 was not adopted by the British Army but was purchased by many other nations, including the Soviet Union. It remains a subject of conjecture as to whether the first Russian amphibious tank was an exact copy of the Vickers type or whether that design was just a source of inspiration. Regardless, the T-37 that was built in 1933 bore a close resemblance to the British original. On the production T-37A, the engine was moved to the rear, allowing the vehicle to be powered by a

Unlike the T-38, the turret on a T-37 was positioned on the right-hand side of the superstructure. The combat value of both types was limited due to them having poor armour protection and limited amphibious performance.

40hp GAZ-AA petrol engine. A small turret mounting a 7.62mm Degtyaryov Tankovy (DT) machine gun, operated by the commander, was positioned to the right of the driver's seat. When waterborne, the vehicle was powered by a propeller mounted on the rear of the hull and steered by a rudder.

After the production of 2,500 T-37A, the T-38 entered production. The main modification was to move the turret from the right-hand side to the left, which made it easily distinguishable from its predecessor.

Both the T-37A and T-38 had relatively similar performance and their armament was considered inadequate. The buoyancy of both was also very poor, being barely sufficient to support the vehicle. However, it should not be forgotten that the Soviet Union was breaking new ground with the large-scale production of amphibious reconnaissance vehicles.

T-40

In 1940, production of a successor to the T-37A/T-38 began. The T-40 had a number of improved essential components. The running gear on the previous types consisted of double bogeys suspended by coil springs, whereas the T-40 had four individual running wheels fitted on internal torsion bars. The use of the latter represented a quantum leap in technology and would become a consistent feature of all future Russian tank developments. The type was powered by an 85hp GAZ 202 engine and had an enlarged hull to improve buoyancy and water-borne performance. The T-40 was armed with a 12.7mm DShK heavy MG and a 7.62mm DT machine gun. Soviet documents indicate that some 220 were produced during World War II.

T-50

In the history of Russian light tanks, the T-50 represents a special case. Developed shortly before the outbreak of World War II, it had similarly revolutionary features as used on the later T-34 medium tank. All sides of the armoured superstructure were sloped, and a 220hp diesel engine gave the 15,000kg vehicle a good power-to-weight ratio. The six-wheel running gear was fitted with torsion bar suspension. The T-60 mounted a proven 45mm 20-K in a ballistically shaped turret that had space for three men and was fitted with a commander's cupola. The type entered service in 1942, but it soon became obvious that the T-50 was almost as difficult to produce as the more powerful T-34 medium tank. Consequently, production was halted after around 70 vehicles had been completed.

The T-40, which entered service in 1939, was also designed as an amphibious tank but with better buoyancy than the earlier T-38. The type was fitted with torsion bar suspension that significantly improved mobility.

T-60

At the same time the T-40 was being developed, so was a conventional light tank. This used many components from the T-40, such as the chassis, engine and transmission, but this new tank, the T-60, would not be amphibious.

The type had superior armament, being fitted with the aircraft-type 20mm TNSh rapid-fire cannon and a 7.62mm DT MG in a co-axial mounting. The hull and superstructure were fabricated from 7mm–20mm armour plate.

When the type entered service in December 1941, it was intended to reduce heavy tank losses until the T-34 and KV were available in greater numbers. But since the 20mm cannon proved to be too weak to defeat the PzKpfw III and PzKpfw IV, the vehicles were increasingly assigned to infantry units for support and reconnaissance tasks. Some 4,500 T-60 light tanks were manufactured during 1942.

T-70

The obvious disadvantages of the T-60 led to the development of a new design. The vehicle was enlarged, requiring the chassis to be extended and a fifth running wheel added. The armour was significantly strengthened; the front plating was now 60mm thick. The vehicle was armed with the proven

45mm 20-K mounted in a turret that made it possible to defeat a PzKpfw III or PzKpfw IV by hitting the sides and rear. The T-70 was powered by two 140hp GAZ-202 petrol engines and it was operated on the battlefront by a crew of two. More than 8,000 were to be built in 1942 and 1943.

The combat value of the T-70 was severely impaired by its small turret, which only had sufficient space for one man, meaning he had to handle all tasks alone during battle. As a result, the T-80 was produced with a larger turret that would accommodate an additional gunner. However, only some 120 were ever produced.

Russia stopped manufacturing light tanks in 1943 to concentrate efforts on the production of the T-34 medium tank, which was seen as crucial to the war and subsequently more important.

It was intended that the hull and running gear of the T-70 would be utilized in the large-scale production of self-propelled guns. In this respect, there is a parallel with the German PzKpfw II.

The most important types were the SU-76 and SU-76M, both of which mounted a 76.2mm ZiS-3 anti-tank gun in an open superstructure. The total number of both types produced is thought to be more than a staggering 14,000 vehicles.

In 1942, the T-70 entered service and was the last Soviet light tank produced in significant numbers during the war. Although it had better armour, armament and mobility, when compared with previous types, its combat value was limited.

United States

After World War I, the general staff of the US military took the decision to disband the US Tank Corps, incorrectly reasoning that another major war was unlikely to occur in future years. What remained of the corps was immediately placed under the command of the infantry. This action followed those of military planners in Great Britain and France. It was not until the early 1930s that the US government ordered the development and production of more modern tanks. Competition with the infantry, who wanted to maintain control of the tank force, slowed the process. In 1940, the US Cavalry also sought to develop a fast tank, but was forced to call its project a 'combat car'.

Combat Car M1

One of the first results of these efforts was the Combat Car M1, which was introduced into the cavalry in 1937.

This tank was planned and built independently, and comprehensively adhered to conventional design practice. First prototypes incorporated a Vickers-type suspension of eight small running wheels with each four carried on a bogey suspended on a large leaf spring. This arrangement was soon superseded by a more effective system that was mounted on the sides of the hull and had two bogeys, each with two running wheels. The running gear was known as Vertical Volute Suspension (VVS) and proved to be far superior to the Vickers type. The track could be tensioned by adjusting the rear idler wheel – a feature that could be found on most US tank types until the end of the war.

The M1 had a combat weight of some 9,000kg and a top speed of over 70kph, and was powered by a 250hp Continental R-670-9A seven-cylinder air-cooled radial petrol engine that was installed at the rear and connected by a shaft to the front-mounted transmission. The R-670 was also used in the Stearman, later Boeing, PT-17 biplane built for the Army Air Corps and US Navy to train fledgling pilots.

The tank was armed with two Browning heavy machine guns – a 0.50in and a 0.30in – installed in a small rotatable turret, as well as another 0.30in, which was available to the radio operator sitting beside the driver. The armour was initially somewhat weak at 6mm–16mm.

The concept was soon to be revised, and as a result, the M2 series was delivered in 1940. Like the M1, the new type was intended to serve as an infantry support tank. Firepower was improved by installing a 37mm Gun M5 main armament. In addition, a 0.50in was mounted at both sides of the front plate. A fifth 0.30in machine gun could be mounted on the turret for anti-aircraft defence.

Opposite: In 1937, the US Cavalry received its first light tank, which was known as the Combat Car M1. The vehicle carried a four-man crew and was armed with a Browning 0.50in heavy MG and two Browning 0.30in MG.

Light Tank M2

Development continued in 1938, and the M1 Combat Car was replaced by the M2 Combat Car, which featured a number of improvements.

As part of fundamental changes to the responsibilities of various branches within the US Army, the cavalry (armoured forces) was, from July 1940, allowed to have tanks. The Combat Car M1 and M2 were renamed Light Tank

In 1940, the Combat Car M1 became the Light Tank M2A4. Armed with a 37mm Gun M1, it provided the US Army with a combat-capable tank. The type was only issued to US forces defending US bases in the Pacific region, here Guadalcanal. (NARA)

M1 and Light Tank M2, and were issued to training units and development trials to help build up the tank force.

After production of small numbers of early variants (M2A1, M2A2 and M2A3), the M2A4 emerged, featuring an extended hull and a more effective 37mm Gun M5 main armament installed in a six-sided turret. The M2A4 was again powered by a Continental R-670-9A engine.

The Light Tank M3 had a better-armoured superstructure, a strengthened chassis and also larger idler wheels that improved driving comfort. The type mounted a 37mm Gun M1 and five 0.30in Browning machine guns.

Light Tank M3

Development of the M2 continued and resulted in the Light Tank M3, which entered service in spring 1940. The frontal armour protection of the now riveted construction was, for a light tank, a remarkable 51mm. The idler wheel was made larger and touched the ground to increase track contact and reduce ground pressure. To save weight on the M3A1, the commander's cupola was removed during production but the type was equipped with attitude stabilization. The side-mounted 0.50in heavy machine guns were omitted. The weight increased to 13,000kg and the top speed reduced to 63kph. Large numbers of almost 14,000 M3 and M3A1 were to be produced. Of those supplied to the British Army, the 1,285 Stuart Mk I (M3) and 213 Stuart Mk IV 213 (M3A1) were powered by a nine-cylinder Guiberson air-cooled radial diesel engine.

Both types were to play a vital role for British units fighting Axis forces in the deserts of North Africa.

Light Tank M5

As a result of further improvements, the Light Tank M5 was created in 1943, replacing the M3 in production. The front of the vehicle was sloped and the armour was increased to 63mm. While this was an improvement, it gave little protection from the ballistic performance of German 5cm KwK L/60 and 7.5cm KwK L/43 tank guns. The type was powered by two 110hp Cadillac V8-cylinder petrol engines, each driving a Hydra-Matic automatic gearbox, which had been developed for use in passenger cars. This combination represented a significant improvement on drivability and the reliability of these components was above average.

The Light Tank M5 entered US Army service in 1942. The type featured all-welded construction and, due to demands for aircraft engines, it was powered by two 110hp Cadillac motorcar engines and automatic transmission. (NARA)

The M5 was, like the M3, primarily used for reconnaissance, a role in which it performed well due to its robustness and mobility. In British service, the M5A1 was known as the Stuart VI. A total of some 9,000 had been produced by June 1944.

Light Tank M24

The experience in North Africa showed that light tanks also had to have an effective offensive armament. The M5 was, within certain limits, capable of fighting the German PzKpfw III and PzKpfw IV, and was therefore increasingly used in the role of a light battle tank.

The installation of a 75mm main gun in a variant of the M3/M5 was not very promising, and the call was made for a new design. These considerations resulted in a new light tank that featured the most modern design yet. In 1943, US industry had both the necessary resources and technical capabilities.

The M24 Chaffee, armed with a 75mm Gun M6, provided US forces with a superior light tank, the chassis of which was to be utilized to build a Light Combat Team series of vehicles. This tank is in service with 30th Division as it pursues the retreating German 116.PzDiv after the failed Ardennes (Battle of the Bulge) offensive. (NARA)

Above Italy 1944: An M24 Chaffee parked alongside a Ford-built M8 Greyhound 6x6 armoured car in a village near Rome. After World War II, the Chaffee was used by US forces in the Korean War and by the Army of the Republic of Vietnam (ARVN) during the Vietnam War. The type was also supplied to more than 30 nations, including those in NATO. Italy alone received more than 500.
(NARA)

The hull and superstructure were of a completely new design and were fabricated by using a welded construction. The front and sides were of a ballistic design that allowed the armour thickness to be reduced to a maximum of 25mm. The type had torsion bar suspension with five large-diameter running wheels.

The new light tank was powered by the same well-proven components as used in the M5; two 110hp Cadillac V8 petrol engines driving robust Hydra-Matic automatic transmission.

As a result, the M-24 Chaffee can be seen as the first modern light combat tank, combining the greatest possible mobility with good firepower and sufficient armour protection. Its contribution to the outcome of World War II is minimal, as it was only used late and in relatively small numbers. Some 4,700 had been built by August 1945, with many remaining in US Army service throughout the Korean War.

The M24 was produced by Cadillac in Detroit, Michigan, and also by Massey-Harris at their facility in Newcastle, Ontario, Canada. Production ended in August 1945 after more than 4,700 had been delivered. (NARA)

Air-portable Tanks

Light Tank Mk VII (A 17) Tetrarch

In 1937, Vickers-Armstrongs began development of the Light Tank Mk VII (A 17) – a larger version of the Mk VI – that was powered by an 8.858cc Meadows MAT/1 flat 12-cylinder petrol engine and fitted with a simplified four-wheel running gear. The type originally mounted an OQF 2-Pounder, but the significantly larger turret allowed a 3in (76.2mm) infantry howitzer to be mounted. The vehicle was subsequently designated as the Tetrarch 1 CS (close support).

In 1941, as a result of *Unternehmen Barbarossa*, 20 Tetrarch were supplied to the Soviet Union under the US/British Lend-Lease Program, but were found to be unsuited to local climatic conditions. Subsequently, the majority were delivered to Red Army tank training schools, but later a few were sent to the battlefront.

The type was first used by British forces, after being landed by ship, during Operation *Ironclad*, the invasion of Madagascar (5 May–6 November 1942).

The Vickers-built Light Tank Mk VII was originally classified as a Light Cruiser Tank by British armoured forces. When the Parachute Regiment was formed in 1942, it required a light tank to provide infantry support. The Mk VII was found to be suitable and entered service as the Tetrarch, but it could only be transported to a landing zone by General Aircraft Hamilcar glider. (Getty)

On 6 June 1944, 20 Tetrarch and their crews, from 6th Airborne Armoured Reconnaissance Regiment, were landed by General Aircraft Hamilcar transport gliders at Ranville, Normandy, as part of the force deployed for Operation *Mallard*. Original British War Office documents indicate that 100 vehicles were ordered.

M22 Locust

In February 1941, representatives of the US Armored Forces and the US Air Force (USAF) demanded the development of an air-transportable tank that was to weigh no more than 7,800kg. Subsequently, the motor manufacturer Marmon-Herrington was contracted to design and build the tank, which had a conventional turret and hull layout. The type was fitted with the mechanically

In 1941, the US Ordnance Board also called for an air-transportable light tank that could be carried by a Douglas C-54 Skymaster. In reality, the M22 was only used by British airborne troops when it was flown into combat by Hamilcar glider. Note the gun is fitted with a Little John Adaptor that reduced the bore from 37mm to 30mm, improving ballistic performance. (NARA)

reliable VVSS suspension and running gear, as used on the M3/M5. To keep within weight limits, a 165hp Lycoming 0-435T six-cylinder, air-cooled petrol engine was selected to power the M22, which had a top speed of 64kph and a range of 217km.

The Locust was armed with a 37mm Gun M6 and a 0.30in Browning M1919A4 machine gun, and carried a crew of three.

Despite being designed to be carried in a cradle fitted under the fuselage of a USAF Douglas C-54 Skymaster transport aircraft, the type was only ever flown in a British-built Hamilcar glider when 22 were deployed for Operation *Varsity* on 24 March 1945.

A total of 830 were completed and 220 were delivered to the British Army under the Lend-Lease Program.

Conclusion 9

The *Panzerwaffe* began its construction in the 1930s, and according to its creator, Heinz Guderian, was intended to become a decisive instrument in any future military conflict.

At that time, German industry lacked both the necessary technical foundations and the industrial potential. Also, for economic reasons, the first types to be introduced in the required large numbers were lightly armoured tanks of small size and low weight.

Under these premises, models such as the PzKpfw I and PzKpfw II were the result of targeted work. Overall, according to the wishes of their creators, these were intended to be a temporary solution until the planned main battle tanks were available in the necessary quantities.

Since the introduction of the PzKpfw III and PzKpfw IV took place after long delays, the older models were expected to remain in use longer than originally planned. The ultimately unplanned integration of the Czechoslovak-built PzKpfw 35(t) and PzKpfw 38(t) could not change this.

The PzKpfw I, which was available in large numbers at the beginning of the war, could only be used to a very limited extent as a combat vehicle, and the PzKpfw II also proved to be only marginally effective in the fight against better-armoured opponents. The possible use of these vehicles in the reconnaissance units was not planned because, according to German doctrine, they were to be equipped with armoured wheeled vehicles only.

The HWa, under the aegis of the engineer Kniepkamp, was to develop modern 'light' tank types before the war began, but due to a lack of industrial capacity, this work was not consistently pursued.

Furthermore, it should not be ignored that the general development of tanks in terms of armament and armour was becoming ever faster; the German developers could not keep up.

Opposite: This PzKpfw I has become immobilized while being driven over marshy terrain. An attempt to drive the vehicle out has caused the left-hand track to break.

The German military planners were aware of the benefits of light tanks. On the one hand, tanks of lower weight could perform many combat tasks better than (heavier) main battle tanks. Furthermore, it should not be underestimated that the parallel production of light tanks would have saved valuable resources. The option to use modern light tank chassis and components for special vehicles, such as self-propelled guns or armoured personnel carriers, was another clear advantage.

Work on such projects began in 1943 and entire series of models were to be developed that, with slight modifications, would be suitable for a wide range of tactical tasks.

The course of the war and the desolate situation of German industry ensured that neither the E series, nor the technically far less demanding Panzer 38 D series, would leave the drawing-board stage.

Germany was ultimately unable to develop a modern light tank.

France 1940: A PzKpfw II, in service with 1.PzDiv, has been positioned to protect a horse-drawn unit as the troops gather to collect their rations from a food truck.

Index

The 15cm sIG 33 was mounted, complete with carriage, on a slightly modified PzKpfw I Ausf B chassis. Note, a *Rundblickfernrohr* (Rbl.F – dial-type) 38 gun sight has been fitted.

The PzKpfw I Ausf A is identified by it having a four-wheel running gear, whereas the Ausf B, being longer, had five. Here, tanks of an unknown battalion prepare to take part in one of the many parades of military strength held before 1939.

Acknowledgements

The author evaluated a vast amount of information that was searched for and found in public archives, including the *Bundesarchiv/Militärarchiv* (BAMA), Freiburg, Germany, and the National Archives & Records Administration (NARA), Washington, USA. An invaluable source was the internet-based project for digitizing German documents in the archives of the Russian Federation. Every document found there was carefully evaluated in the context of its historical background and represents a significant portion of the book.

The technical aspects of the German light tanks have been extensively evaluated in the *Panzer Tracts* series of publications produced by the late Thomas Jentz and Hilary L. Doyle, which I recommend for further information. I also used books written by Walter J. Spielberger as a source and inspiration. Other post-war publications were used only to a limited extent.

My sincere thanks to the following individuals who granted me access to their collections: Florian von Aufseß, Holger Erdmann, Karlheinz Münch and Henry Hoppe. Also, to Hilary Doyle for the use of his excellent line drawings of the Panzer 38(D). Finally, my gratitude to Rauno Vaara, archivist at the Swedish Army Museum, Stockholm, Sweden, and Nils Erik Nilsson at the Garrison Museum, Skaraborg, Sweden, for images of the Stridsvagn m/21 and m/31.

Thanks to my editor, Jasper Spencer-Smith, that ever-patient gentleman, for his for guidance and work on my manuscript and the completed book. Also, thanks to Justin Smith for his carefully prepared page layout.

All images in this book are, unless otherwise credited, from the Thomas Anderson Collection.

Bibliography

Doyle, H & Jentz. T: *Panzer Tracts*, various editions – Panzer Tracts, Boyds, ML, USA.

Guderian, H: *Erinnerungen eines Soldaten*, first edition – Kurt Voßwinckel Verlag, Heidelberg, Germany.

Jentz, T: *Die Deutschen Panzertruppen*, Volumes 1 & 2 – Podzun-Pallas Verlag, Wölfersheim, Germany.

Nehring, W: *Die Geschichte der Deutschen Panzerwaffe* 1916 bis 1945 – Motorbuch Verlag, Stuttgart, Germany.